One Nation Under-Taught

Solving America's Science, Technology, Engineering & Math Crisis

Dr. Vince M. Bertram

Beaufort Books
New York

Library of Congress Cataloging-in-Publication Data on file

ISBN: 9780825307447

For inquiries about volume orders, please contact:

Beaufort Books
27 West 20th Street, Suite 1102
New York, NY 10011
sales@beaufortbooks.com

Published in the United States by Beaufort Books
www.beaufortbooks.com

Distributed by Midpoint Trade Books
www.midpointtrade.com

Printed in the United States of America

Interior design by Vally Sharpe

Educate and inform the whole masses...They are the only sure reliance of the preservation of our liberty.
—*Thomas Jefferson*—

Contents

Foreword

by Steve Forbes

As a nation, we have known for decades that our K-12 education system is in serious trouble, that our students routinely lag their counterparts in numerous other countries in language and mathematical skills. This is especially worrisome in an era in which high tech is becoming more and more critically important for advancing economically. That millions of our children are not being taught effectively—or at all—in the crucial areas of science, technology, engineering and math, popularized by the acronym STEM, is a moral outrage. Their opportunities to get ahead, to "improve their lot in life," as Abraham Lincoln put it, are being seriously harmed and our future well-being as a nation is being jeopardized.

Thankfully, America has a tradition dating back to Colonial times of not being passive when serious challenges arise. Vince Bertram is a splendid example of this can-do, let's-roll-up-our-sleeves-and-do-something-about-it characteristic. His organization, Project Lead The Way (PLTW), has been tackling the STEM deficiencies in our primary and secondary schools for a decade and a half. PLTW has become the leading provider in the U.S. of STEM programs for kids in grades K-12. In addition to coming up with world-class curriculums Dr. Bertram and his colleagues have created superb professional development programs for teachers. More than 6,000 schools around the country have benefitted from PLTW's crucial work.

Dr. Bertram understands that it's not enough to come up with solutions, that you must also actively work with students, parents, teachers, administrators, parents, universities, businesses and foundations, as well as community and government leaders to affect lasting, positive change. Interacting with all parties—brainstorming, if you will—can also generate new ideas on how to move forward.

While PLTW has made powerful contributions, so much more remains to be done throughout the nation. Hence, the crying need for Vince Bertram's new book. It couldn't be more timely, as recognition of our STEM educational deficits is growing. Dr. Bertram brings immense knowledge and expertise to the subject and speaks from frontline experience.

Dr. Bertram lays out the irrefutable evidence of the crisis: of how, since the mid-1960s, American students have been slipping in what they actually learn in our schools, especially in the STEM fields. According to the National Assessment of Education Progress, only 26 percent of American high school seniors in 2010 scored at or above the proficiency level in math. More ominously, a staggering 36 percent had failing scores. Worse, only 3 percent scored at an advanced level in math, and a pitiful 1percent in science.

No wonder so few U.S.-educated high school students go on to pursue STEM courses in college. No wonder our high-tech centers, epitomized by Silicon Valley, must recruit literally hundreds of thousands of foreign-educated people to try to fulfill their needs for skill-based workforces. Even with that, huge gaps remain, which is why companies have to set up facilities overseas to meet their requirements.

All of which, of course, begs the question: Why don't our schools do a better job?

It's not as if we don't know we have an enormous problem. Back in 1983, the state of education had gotten so bad that the then relatively new Department of Education released a report titled "A Nation at Risk." The ominous opening words from that report were powerful and tough and are worth re-quoting at length:

Our Nation is at risk. Our once unchallenged preeminence in commerce, industry, science, and technological innovation is being overtaken by competitors throughout the world. This report is concerned with only one of the many causes and dimensions of the problem, but it is the one that undergirds American prosperity, security, and civility. We report to the American people that ... the educational foundations of our society are being presently eroded by a rising tide of mediocrity that threatens our very future as a Nation and a people. What was unimaginable a generation ago has begun to occur—others are matching and surpassing our educational attainments.

If an unfriendly foreign power had attempted to impose on America the mediocre educational performance that exists today, we might well have viewed it as an act of war. As it stands, we have allowed this to happen to ourselves. We have even squandered the gains in student achievement made in the wake of the Sputnik challenge. Moreover, we have dismantled essential support systems which helped make those gains possible. We have, in effect, been committing an act of unthinking, unilateral educational disarmament.

Our society and its educational institutions seem to have lost sight of the basic purposes of schooling, and of the high expectations and disciplined effort needed to attain them.

Alas, while we have poured immense sums into our education bureaucracies, these increased resources have had little or no effect. We experimented with reforms that were as bad in conception as they were in reality. And we continued to adjust down to mediocrity—or worse. As those numbers from the National Assessment of Education Progress attest, our students' scores over the past generations have been, as education expert Chester Finn Jr. put it, "Flat, flat, flat."

We largely failed in fighting back against this "rising tide of mediocrity." Mediocrity does not sustain itself: One is either advancing or sliding backward. It's been said that what goes on in a nation's classrooms will eventually work its way up to a nation's governance and economy. We see that, we live with that today.

Of course, we have pockets of excellence in some of our nation's schools—Dr. Bertram and his team have been immensely helpful here. But they are pockets, not the norm. Too many of our students drop out of STEM fields, seeing them as boring or too difficult, and this aversion starts in the early elementary grades.

It's here that we get to what makes Dr. Bertram's book such a timely gem and an exciting contribution. Vince Bertram does far more than lament our predicament. He provides a blueprint for enabling students to fall in love with STEM subjects—subjects that don't have to be dreary or intimidating. He shows how teachers can break away from the rut of traditional teaching and kindle in kids that inspiring curiosity that will lead them to becoming passionate about learning.

Dr. Bertram is no armchair reformer. He's been in the trenches as a teacher, principal and superintendent. Through PLTW he has implemented programs that actually work. And, very importantly, his programs have equipped teachers with the intellectual and practical tools necessary to teach STEM subjects well. Students quickly come to see the true relevance of these subjects in today's world. They become inspired.

This is why we, as a nation, must "ramp up" the kinds of reforms Dr. Bertram and his colleagues have so successfully put into practice. The time for talk and ineffectual actions is long, long past. Vince Bertram shows us the way.

Author's Note

When problems arise, many people are inclined to blame someone or something. This book is not about assigning blame. It is about clearly articulating the problem and taking responsibility to solve it.

We have many highly effective educators who are doing extraordinary work with students; local, state, and federal policymakers who care deeply about their communities, states, and country; mission-driven non-profit organizations working to enhance the lives of those they serve; and businesses striving to win in a highly competitive global marketplace. But, despite all these efforts, we are falling behind in educating our youth and our future workforce and we must do something about it.

This is a different kind of business and education book than most may be used to, and it is not just about science, technology, engineering, and math (STEM). Those subjects are a series of courses or disciplines. This book is about the importance of those subjects, yes, but, more: it is a book about how we integrate and use STEM knowledge. It is about how we inspire a thirst for STEM education. It is also a book about American greatness and our economy. This book is a call to action: asking teachers, principals, counselors, parents, business and community leaders to impart knowledge and experiences they may very well not have had themselves.

This is a call to nurture our children's natural curiosity, inspire them, and insist they use their minds to solve problems. This book asks us to rethink the way we think about school. It asks that we abandon the mindset that second grade is a preparation for third grade or of teaching content merely to prepare for a test. Instead, I am asking for a new mindset about school, a mindset that our schools can be places of confidence, places that inspire a love of learning, promote curiosity, and convince students that skills and knowledge matter—not because they are on a test or necessary for the next year, but because they matter for a lifetime.

I wrote this book because I believe if we do not change our present course, we are preparing too many of our children—and too many in our country—for a lifetime of poverty. That is why we must be realistic and tell our children, and our graduating high school and college seniors, the truth. Commencement addresses at these graduations are rife with advice telling students to "follow your dreams"—this is often misguided advice, often very bad advice. For us to live in a world where this advice were applicable or led to success, there would need to be a lot more jobs for professional athletes and Broadway performers. The reality is, dreams may be incongruous with real job prospects, with simple reality. For example, throughout school, many children spend their evenings at sports practice, and even more nights dreaming of being a professional athlete. However, ninety-nine percent don't make it.

It sounds harsh, but it is the reality. Only a very small percentage of students will ever play in the NFL. In fact, according to Business Insider and the National Collegiate Athletic Association (NCAA), only 1.7 percent of college football players will play in the NFL, and only 1.2 percent and 0.9 percent of basketball players go on to play in the NBA and WNBA, respectively. This is of those who make it to the NCAA in the first place. The best opportunity is baseball, which Business Insider/NCAA reports offers an 11.6 percent chance for college athletes to go pro (for many, that means playing years in the farm system, hoping to be called up to the major league). And it's not just athletics. The same small percentages apply to music and the arts—Adele and J.K. Rowling are exceedingly rare talents, and so were Pablo Picasso and Frédéric Chopin.

So what do we tell our kids? We tell them to pursue their passions, whatever those passions might be—the arts, music, sports—because you never know who might be talented and lucky enough to make it to the big leagues. We also need to be honest with our children and tell them that while they can choose which path to take, others will likely decide whether they will get paid to do it. Life will be easier—much easier—if they have the appropriate skills aligned with the greatest opportunities.

So in what fields will students find the greatest potential for success? Forbes highlights the most in-demand college majors— the fields that will present our graduates with the most job prospects and highest earnings. Engineering and math fields dominated the list, with engineering concentrations making up one-third of the most valuable majors. Biomedical engineering ranked #1; software engineering was #4, followed by environmental engineering (#5), civil engineering (#6), and petroleum engineering (#7).

These findings are nothing new, however. I've written often about the issues the STEM skills gap is creating and how they greatly threaten America's economic competitiveness. By 2018, STEM jobs are expected to grow at a rate nearly double that of other fields—17 percent versus 9.8 percent. An estimated 1.2 million STEM jobs will go unfilled because the workforce will not possess the skills to fill them. And, as the world continues to innovate and as new technologies emerge every day, the jobs gap will widen. So what can we do?

The answer is clear. We must reach our students earlier, introduce them to math and science, and show them the engaging, exciting, and practical applications of those subjects. We must continue to foster curiosity and collaboration, critical thinking and problem-solving skills, and stress to our students that the purpose of education is to prepare for the global economy, an economy that is demanding more graduates with STEM knowledge and skills. We must counsel our students from an early age, introduce them to available career options, and guide them on the path to pursue those careers with the appropriate course work and activities. We must encourage our students to begin thinking about their careers long before they finish high school.

The bottom line is this. Students should continue to pursue their passions and the dream of becoming the next Peyton Manning or LeBron James. But let's also set them up with a solid foundation for a successful and stable life just in case the scouts don't call. And if your child or student does end up within that rare .08 percent of athletes who go pro, a strong academic foundation will give them security. Studies show that within two years of retirement, seventy-eight percent of former NFL players have gone bankrupt or are under financial stress. We must help our children have a brighter future through a career they can pursue once their dream career ends. And for the other group—the majority 99.02 percent—opening their eyes to the career possibilities of their future will excite them and inspire them, and give them a new dream to pursue. A dream that leads to a successful life.

Like many of my colleagues, I was attracted to education because of influential people in my life who inspired me to be more than I thought I possibly could be. Now, we need to be that inspiration for millions of children across our great nation.

This book is about the problem and the solution. Let's go to work.

One Nation
Under-Taught

1

Failing Ourselves

In 2013, the National Assessment of Educational Progress (or NAEP, known as "The Nation's Report Card") revealed that only twenty-six percent of our nation's twelfth graders were scoring at or above proficient in math while thirty-five percent were failing.[1] To put it another way, almost forty percent of Americans about to enter the workforce, military, college, and achieving voting age do so unable to perform basic mathematics. That is, they cannot, among other things, "compute, approximate, and estimate with real numbers" or "order and compare real numbers and perform routine arithmetic calculations with and without a scientific calculator or spreadsheet."[2]

Here, astoundingly to me, is a sample question from a recent NAEP math test for high school seniors, a sample question nearly forty percent of our nation's seniors got wrong:

$$360 \text{ x } .03 =$$
a) 10.8
b) 108
c) 120
d) 980
e) 1,080[3]

Almost fifteen percent of the respondents selected answer "d" or "e," which is to say almost fifteen percent of our nation's high school students thought three percent of 360 was a number greater than 360.

The larger point here is that the state of American STEM education is not good. Indeed, it is terrible. As a result, we are depriving millions of children the opportunity for productive and great careers, and depriving our country the workforce and brain-power we need. We are in crisis—a crisis that it is imperiling our future economy and position in the world.

This is not to say that good STEM teachers, students, or programs do not exist. They do. What I am saying is that, as a general matter, our country is failing our students and itself. Consider a few more statistics.

In measuring our fifteen-year-olds against their peers in other Organization for Economic Cooperation and Development (OECD) countries in the field of science in 2012, our students came in twenty-first, below such countries as Estonia, Poland, and Ireland.[4] In measuring our fifteen-year-olds against peers in other OECD countries in the field of math, our students came in twenty-sixth, below such countries as Liechtenstein, Iceland, and the Czech Republic.[5] Over and over again, the places that come in at the top? Shanghai, Singapore, Taiwan, South Korea, and Japan. Upon the release of these rankings and scores, the *Wall Street Journal* editorialized: "Perhaps most depressingly, the data show no statistically significant U.S. achievement improvement over time. None. In an era when it pays to be thankful for small mercies, at least we're not getting worse, but America's relative standing is falling as other countries improve."[6]

While every test has its critics, the OECD test, known as the "Program for International Student Assessment" (or PISA), is highly respected. U.S. Secretary of Education Arne Duncan said of the results from the 2009 test, which showed results similar to those of the 2012 test, "We can quibble, or we can face the brutal truth that we're being out-educated."[7] Secretary Duncan is right, but he could go further. We are being out-educated because we are simply not realizing our potential. We are a nation under-taught and under-educated. The fault is ours.

When it comes to our own scores at home, the news looks even worse. NAEP, as mentioned above, measures our students in a variety of subjects at different grade levels; it is administered to hundreds of thousands of students in America and is known as "the gold standard" of testing. Almost all education experts hold it in high regard.[8] In the most recent assessment of fourth and eighth graders, released in 2013, we found that only thirty-four percent of our nation's fourth graders were "proficient" at math—that is, they were at an achievement level one would think of as "competent" or higher—and seventeen percent were "below basic" in their mathematics abilities. In other words, almost one out of five fourth graders were failing math.[9] By eighth grade, the numbers were even worse: twenty-seven percent of our nation's eighth graders were performing at the proficient level while a full twenty-six percent were scoring below basic, or failing.[10] By high school, as we saw above, the numbers were worse yet.[11]

Given all the resources we have at our disposal today, given all the money we pour into school systems (over $600 billon a year in America in elementary and secondary education funding alone) and into studies on how to educate, it is nothing short of tragic that a majority of our nation's students score below a standard of competence, or proficient. Looking at the trend where fourth graders score better than eighth graders, who score better than twelfth graders, former U.S. Secretary of Education and Project Lead The Way (PLTW) Senior Advisor William J. Bennett observes: "The longer one stays in school in America, the worse one does."[12]

When it comes to science education, we do dismally as well. In fourth grade, the latest NAEP scores (from 2009) show a thirty-four percent proficiency rate and a twenty-eight percent failure rate.[13] In eighth grade, the most recent NAEP (from 2011) reveals thirty-two percent of our students scoring proficiently and thirty-five percent failing.[14] And our twelfth graders? The most recent assessment for them (2009) shows a twenty-one percent proficiency rate and a full forty percent failure rate[15]—worse than they do in math and, still, an upside-down trajectory where the longer students stay in school, the worse they perform.

The state of our STEM education does not have to be this way, but more importantly, it cannot stay this way. The good news is, while there is rampant failure and mediocrity throughout our nation's education system, there are great examples where this is simply not happening, where success is the norm. However, if America is going to remain the—or just a—leading nation, we must ignite a fierce urgency throughout our nation's education system. We must move from pockets of excellence to a system of excellence.

To highlight the need for this fierce urgency, we only need go to the most recent White House report from the President's Council of Advisors on Science and Technology (or PCAST). The President's Council opened its February 2012 report stating, "Economic projections point to a need for approximately one million more STEM professionals than the U.S. will produce at the current rate over the next decade if the country is to retain its historical preeminence in science and technology. To meet this goal, the United States will need to increase the number of students who receive undergraduate STEM degrees by about thirty-four percent annually over current rates."[16] We are not on course to do this - not at the elementary, secondary, or post-secondary levels of education.

This is a challenging proposition given our students' lack of interest and poor performance in science and math. A recent report suggested that about twenty-eight percent of high school freshmen (one million high school students) declare an interest in STEM-related fields each year, but some fifty-seven percent of them will lose interest over the course of their high school careers.[17] We lose about 570,000 STEM-eager high school students each year by their senior year in high school. We are turning off over half a million brains to the fields of math and science in high school alone...every year!

And, nowhere near a majority of high school students are even competent in subjects like math and science, never mind advanced. Only three percent of our nation's high school seniors score at an "advanced" level in math on the NAEP test,[18] while only one percent of our nation's high school seniors score at an "advanced" level in science.[19] A portion of these are the students who most likely will go on to attain graduate degrees in those fields, attend the best colleges and universities in those fields, and ultimately go on to become leaders in their fields in academics, medicine, research, or industry. One recent report puts that portion at about seventeen percent![20]

So, by the time we have high school seniors competent in science and math, and still interested in STEM fields and careers, we have a woefully inadequate pool or pipeline. Then they get to college. And there, less than forty percent of college students who enter college intent on a degree in the STEM fields stay on course and graduate with that STEM degree.[21] We lose students' interest in high school if we were fortunate enough to have encouraged those students in elementary and middle school in the first place; and then of those who stay interested, we lose a majority of them in college.

We simply cannot go on this way, not if the serious reports on the future needs of this country are to be taken seriously, and they should be. The current STEM workforce is about 7.4 million employees with an estimated 8.6 million employees needed by 2018.[22] And that is just a minimum projection. America cannot win by simply maintaining the number of students who pursue STEM-related degrees; we need to inspire over one million more, and that is just to stay the course with the current economy. But, we are not on that trajectory. We are nowhere near it.

2

The American Economy of Today and Tomorrow—Still the Last Best Hope?

Abraham Lincoln famously declared the United States "the last, best hope of earth." Other leaders have said much the same in the past. Ronald Reagan put his twist on it by calling us "the last, best hope of man on earth."[23] The Russian human rights hero and Nobel laureate Aleksandr Solzhenitsyn said, "The United States of America has long shown itself to be the most magnanimous, the most generous country in the world."[24] And in his time, the novelist Thomas Wolfe said America "is a fabulous country, the only fabulous country; it is the only place where miracles not only happen, but where they happen all the time."[25] I could go on and on with these kinds of quotes about American greatness. But what all the giants of leadership and letters were testifying to was not just our nation's political philosophy, dedicated to liberty and equality as it was and is. They were speaking to the significance of the equal opportunity and freedom that had led us and the world, in their time and before, and could continue to lead us in the future. This notion of "best hope," or greatness of national and international leadership, of exceptionalism, can only continue to apply and abide if America is to remain an economic powerhouse—if it continues to be a place of industry, financial strength, growth, employment, startups, innovation, and entrepreneurship.

But the fundamentals of our economy today are not strong; indeed, they bode serious trouble and concern. Let us take a look at the landscape of our recent recession and state of economic affairs. Most people over the age of fifty can remember the 1970s, or what is loosely referred to as the "Carter years," as a time of economic hardship and failure. The standard line that then-governor Ronald Reagan used in talking about unemployment in his campaign against President Jimmy Carter in those years was: "A recession is when your neighbor loses his job. A depression is when you lose yours. And recovery is when Jimmy Carter loses his."[26] Ronald Reagan got a lot of mileage out of that line. But for as bad as our economy and the state of unemployment was in those years, the numbers are almost enviable when contrasted to today.[27]

The highest unemployment rate in the Carter years, the late 1970s, was 7.5 percent and by 1979 unemployment was in the five-percent-to-six-percent range.[28] When the American economy went into free-fall in 2008—President George W. Bush's last year in office—and the presidential campaign became so much about the economy, unemployment was heading toward seven percent again (after it had been in the four-percent- and five-percent-range for many of the previous years).[29] When President Barack Obama took office in 2009, unemployment was already at 7.8 percent and would surge up to eight, nine, and then ten percent.[30]

When the "Recovery Summer" was declared by the Obama administration in 2010, unemployment was still over nine percent. Through the summer of 2013, America was showing the worst GDP growth rate for a full fifteen quarters since World War II.[31] And today, with a rate still over six percent, many do not believe this is the real unemployment rate, given how many Americans are underemployed or have simply stopped looking for work. Some have argued the real unemployment rate may be as high as fourteen percent or greater.[32] This is double the rate than when most Americans thought the economy was in terrible shape.

Other fundamentals today reveal an equally worrisome landscape. Our economic growth, measured in Gross Domestic Product (or GDP), stood at about 2.3 percent over the last few years.[33] While that is better than no growth, or "negative growth," it is still an anemic number. By contrast, in the 1950s, there were years with seven percent and eight percent growth; in the 1960s we had years with five percent and six percent growth, in the 1970s and 1980s, we had years with over five percent and sometimes seven percent growth, but now we are lucky to get up to 2.3 percent GDP growth.[34] And, as recently as June of 2014, the *Wall Street Journal* had this headline: "U.S. Economy Shrinks by Most in Five Years."[35] Yes, with all the talk of "recovery," indeed it truly runs weak to sporadic with one step forward and two steps back. To give a little more of an idea on how this is occurring, here's more from the story:

> Gross domestic product, the broadest measure of goods and services produced across the economy, fell at a seasonally adjusted annual rate of 2.9% in the first quarter, the Commerce Department said in its third reading of the data Wednesday.
>
> That was a sharp downward revision from the previous estimate that output fell at an annual rate of 1%. It also represented the fastest rate of decline since the recession, and was the largest drop recorded since the end of World War II that wasn't part of a recession.[36]

Growth is what both encourages and indicates innovation and overall economic health. We simply are not healthy today. Indeed, we are, as of this writing, in the summer of 2014, just coming out of a first quarter contraction![37] I fear we may be forgetting what "healthy" looks and feels like.

This is all much more than troubling. Take a look at our average high school or college senior. Assuming high school or college graduation in the first place (which is a topic of concern I will address later): What are our seniors' job prospects? What are his or her opportunities? While today's student debt is at an all-time high, surpassing one trillion dollars, with many struggling to pay off that debt, many believe that number alone could constitute the next economic bubble to burst.[38] But the outlook was discouraging for 2013 graduates. A Google scan of news headlines: "College Grads Overconfident in Job Prospects,"[39] "Job Picture Looks Bleak for 2013 College Grads,"[40] "The Class of 2013: Young Graduates Still Face Dim Job Prospects,"[41] "Half of College Grads Can't Find Full-time Work…"[42] And these headlines came as the 2013 market was actually better than the 2012 market.

Where, however, is there a potential bright spot? According to a report by the National Association of Colleges and Employers, "employment areas with the greatest demand for this year's graduates include business, engineering, computer sciences and accounting."[43] But this is only a potential bright spot because while there is demand, there is not supply:

> A survey of 500 hiring managers by recruitment firm Adecco, found that a majority—66 percent—believe new college graduates are not prepared for the workforce after leaving college. Fifty-eight percent said they were not planning to hire entry-level graduates this year, and among those managers hiring, 69 percent said they plan to bring on only one or two candidates.
>
> "Too many students are graduating with a weak background in science and math," said Mauri Ditzler, president of Monmouth College.
>
> "We need to make sure our graduates know the basics and many don't."[44]

Graduates do not know the basics in the areas where there is and will be actual job growth and demand. And those are the "graduates." The drop-outs have an even poorer shot at the American dream, a sad commentary given that we have a forty-three percent college graduation rate in America, placing us eleventh among the OECD list of countries.[45] As for high school graduation? One million high school students a year drop out, "a loss of 5,500 students for every day on the academic calendar."[46]

There is a healthy, ongoing debate in our country about the actual economic worth of a college education, and many of my friends and colleagues have important and diverse views on the subject. But, three things are indisputable: 1) high school completion is simply not enough; 2) if you want to dramatically increase your options for gainful and sustainable employment—even in a down economy with bleak job prospects—the odds are heavily tilted toward those with a college or advanced degree; and, 3) the types of skills, knowledge, and degrees matter.

The odds are simply better with degrees in "business, engineering, computer sciences, and accounting," or what many call or label "the hard sciences." Even most of my friends who question the worth of college education do not question it in those fields or for those who go to top colleges. The entrepreneurial geniuses Bill Gates and Steve Jobs, who dropped out of college to create vast empires, are the rare exceptions. As William Bennett and David Wilezol stated in *Is College Worth It?*, "If you are accepted into the Colorado School of Mines, Harvey Mudd, Stanford, Plan II at the University of Texas, and dozens of other places...then go. And if you want to study petroleum engineering or any kind of engineering and have an aptitude for it, then go."[47]

But therein lies the problem: aptitude. Not enough of our high school students are ready or even interested in post-secondary education like that. There is a reason, after all, that so many high tech companies and chambers of commerce want to expand the number of H1B visas granted every year in America. The H1B visa is the high-skilled non-immigrant work visa, especially common in the areas of engineering and math.[48] So badly are these workers needed that one recent report found that "in the absence of green cards and H1B visa constraints in the 2003-07 period, roughly

182,000 foreign graduates of U.S. colleges and universities would likely have remained in the country and raised the gross domestic product (GDP) by roughly $13.6 billion."[49] By the way, the vast majority of the H1B visas go to students from Asia, mostly China and Korea—no great surprise given the numbers I presented in the opening of this book.[50] More than half of the science and engineering graduates working in America today are from other countries.[51]

Of the nearly 1.8 million bachelor degrees awarded in America each year, only about one-third are in STEM-related fields, while a majority of China's bachelor degrees and over sixty percent of Japan's bachelor degrees are in those fields.[52] "South Korea graduates more engineers than the United States…and in many Asian countries, 21 percent of college graduates are engineers, compared to 12 percent in Europe and 4.5 percent in the United States," reported Charles Vest, president of the National Academy of Engineering and MIT president emeritus.[53]

I write "so badly are these workers needed," above because of reports just like this one, showing that we simply are not raising our own graduates able to take these jobs and boost our GDP. I support expanding the H1B visa program, but I do so knowing the tragedy of the decision: we do not train our own students well enough to take these jobs and raise our GDP. In other words, it is both a shame and a necessity that we have to import talent. I am, however, an optimist, supporting the expanded visa program on a temporary basis, because I firmly believe we can reverse course and, in fact, "grow our own." Indeed, I know that if we are to remain the last best hope of earth, we have no other choice. We cannot survive on temporary and imported talent forever, we cannot consign our own citizens and children to average and less than average educations any longer, and certainly not at the same time other nations are beating us.

This is not just a matter of education for education's sake or for the mere desire and preference that we employ our own citizens while unemployment is high instead of having to import from other countries the talent our own corporations need. No. This is about staying competitive in the global economy and not allowing any country to beat us as an economic and education engine or powerhouse. I am not an expert in international economics or in international relations, nor is this book focused on those topics, but it does not take such an expert to tell us that we need to be concerned about our own economy for our own sake, and that we need to be concerned about our competition.

I believe it is fair to say that the last several presidential administrations—both Republican and Democratic—have viewed China as an economic competitor and certainly a large portion of the world does as well. A recent Pew Global Attitudes survey found, for instance, that "53 percent in Britain said China is the leading economy, while 33 percent name the U.S. In Germany, 59 percent say China occupies the top place, while only 19 percent think the U.S is the global economic leader."[54] And here, in America? What do we think of ourselves? We are not so sure, but we are thinking less and less of ourselves compared to China: "Americans are divided, with 47 percent saying that China has or will replace the U.S. and 47 percent saying this will never happen. That is a significant shift of U.S. public opinion from 2008 when only 36 percent said China would become the top global power and 54 percent said China would never replace the U.S."[55]

One can certainly make the case, as many have, that China's days as an economic powerhouse are numbered for several reasons. But there are a few indisputable facts that still remain, aside from China's education prowess and achievements (especially as compared to our own): The Chinese economy is the second largest in the world, and as one economic respondent to the prognosticators of China's collapse put it:

[W]hile China's economy may slow to less than the 8-10 percent growth it normally averages, a real collapse, to growth rates of 2 percent or 3 percent, or less, is highly unlikely. For one, China's state and private companies may be getting too easy credit from state banks, but that does not mean these businesses are actually unproductive, like some of the Thai and Indonesian companies caught up in the 1997 Asian finance crisis. The truly unproductive Chinese state-owned and state-linked enterprises were closed down more than a decade ago....

Meanwhile:

Chinese companies alone, nearly all of them state-owned, occupied 73 of the top 500 slots in Fortune's 2012 ranking of the largest companies in the world by sales. China's score has steadily risen on the Global Competitiveness Index; the World Economic Forum's ranking of nations' international economic competitiveness. And several Chinese companies, such as Huawei, have come to dominate global markets like telecommunications.[56]

As of this writing, China's economic growth rate has, indeed, slowed, to between 7.4 and 7.5 percent. The United States is stuck at about 2.8 percent growth, on average, over the past few years with very little prospect of the optimists' hope that we reach an annual three percent growth by the end 2014.[57] As for their education condition, education expert Chester E. Finn, Jr., said this after seeing China's international rankings in reading, math, and science: "Wow, I'm kind of stunned....I've seen how relentless the Chinese are at accomplishing goals, and if they can do this in Shanghai in 2009, they can do it in 10 cities in 2019, and in 50 cities by 2029."[58] In all my travels throughout America, and having visited hundreds of schools, I have never heard an American education official look at a successful system in America and say without a doubt that we can replicate such success in fifty cities (too often, I do hear reasons why isolated examples of success are not replicable). It is my proposal and theory, however, that we can replicate success. I certainly know we must.

With over $600 billion a year invested in public elementary and secondary education,[59] Americans spend more than any other developed nation on its K-12 school students.[60] But we are falling behind too many of those other nations—investing money in programs that add little or no value and not appropriately educating our youth. Why do other countries, particularly Asian countries in the STEM fields, continually beat us? The reasons are myriad...but, I'm convinced the solutions are not. I have the privilege to see how rigorous programs in STEM education can transform not only students' minds, but our educational landscape as well—from theory to action. We just need to take what we know works to scale.

It is in the STEM fields where that need is most urgent. That is where the growth and opportunities are. It is also where our international counterparts are most seriously beating us. But do not just take my word for it. The Nobel Prize-winning economist Robert Solow has pointed out that half the economic growth in America since World War II has come from advances in science and technology.[61] Susan Hockfield, President of the Massachusetts Institute of Technology (MIT), made two key points on this recently: Asking, "What can we do, together, to restart America's job-creation machine?" she said,

> I believe the answer lies in retooling the engine that has driven wave after wave of economic growth since the end of World War II: America's innovation system....Our innovation system comes to life from the spark of scientific discovery and invention — but the kind of innovation that drives real economic growth goes beyond a cool idea or an incremental improvement on an old practice or product. We're driving for innovations that produce big new ideas, based in science or technology, that can be transformed into market-ready products. Innovations that can create new markets — sometimes even new industries — and that create a future different from, and better than, the present.[62]

She also warned us about our ability to deliver on those innovations: "If we want to make U.S. jobs, we can't just make ideas here — we have to make the products here. Unfortunately, no amount of innovation will be enough if we ship all of our manufacturing abroad. America remains the world's second-largest manufacturer, but with so many nations copying our innovation model, we must stake our bets on the kind of advanced manufacturing the future demands."[63] This statement, alone, haunts me as I digest all that has gone wrong with the city of Detroit, once known not only as the automobile manufacturing capital of the world but once even as the "Capital of the 20th Century." Today it is, literally, bankrupt. I believe, however, if Detroit's bankruptcy is to be overcome, it will be overcome by innovation and growth such as what GM has done to turn itself around from bankruptcy, and not simply because of government investment.[64] In fact, speaking of his company's resurgence, former GM CEO Dan Akerson responded to a congressional delegation, "no, we're fine," when asked if Washington should provide more help.[65]

Others, from industry, have weighed in on the importance of STEM as well. Fred Smith, the Founder and Chairman of FedEx has stated, "I personally think that the federal government—and you're talking to a liberal arts major here—should restrict its funding of higher-education grants and loans to science, math, and engineering because that's where most of the value added comes."[66] Rodney C. Adkins, a senior vice president at IBM has written, "When I graduated from college [circa 1978], about 40% of the world's scientists and engineers resided in the U.S. Today that number has shrunk to about 15%."[67] Antonio Perez, chairman and CEO of Eastman Kodak put it this way: "The American economy has always depended on innovation, and in a knowledge-based society, there can be no real innovation without an educational emphasis on science, technology, engineering and math. This is especially important to create a workforce that can succeed in today's rapidly changing economy."[68]

I could go on and on with a list of quotes along these lines. But, there is a reason dozens of corporate leaders in America, from companies as diverse as Chevron, Lockheed Martin, Dow Chemical, Eli Lilly, GE, and Facebook have formed Change the Equation, a "CEO-led initiative that is mobilizing the business community to improve the quality of science, technology, engineering and mathematics learning in the United States."[69] This is a critically important organization helping sound the clarion call and proposing solutions to our STEM education problems in America. Change the Equation, led by Linda Rosen, recently endorsed four high quality and nationally scalable organizations: Project Lead The Way, Gilstart Summer Camp, ST Math, and Ten80 Student Racing Challenge. We ignore its work at our peril. I encourage every reader of this book to check out its website.

But, for now, to highlight as simply as possible the economic challenge and opportunity we face with STEM education, let me go to a recent report from PCAST. The report is essential reading. "Throughout the 20th century, the U.S. education system drove much of our Nation's economic growth and prosperity," the Council states.[70] Obvious enough. And if not obvious enough, it states what I have been trying to highlight in this chapter: "Despite our historical record of achievement, the United States now lags behind other nations in STEM education at the elementary and secondary levels. Over the past several decades, a variety of indicators have made clear that we are failing to educate many of our young people to compete in an increasingly high-tech global economy and to contribute to national goals."[71]

STEM is where the growth is needed and STEM is where our economic growth is. As the Chancellor of the University of Wisconsin-Madison, Rebecca Blank, posited when she was working in the Department of Commerce, "STEM workers earn a premium of 25 percent over other workers and have only a 5.5 percent unemployment rate."[72] These numbers are backed up by other reports, including a recent one by the National Governors'

Association, which further pointed out that while the 5.5 percent unemployment rate applied to STEM workers, it hit ten percent at the same time for non-STEM workers.[73] In fact, the chances of one being unemployed in a STEM field are exceedingly rare as STEM job postings actually outnumber unemployed people.[74]

William Bennett and David Wilezol point out why this is; and while it may say something good about interest in some of the humanities and liberal arts fields, the basic realities of the economy tell a different tale: "Too many students gravitate toward majors in which they gain few skills or for which there is little workplace demand."[75] I will later go into some of the reasons why there is a crisis in our major fields of studies, but first it is worth pointing out that while total college enrollment has risen some fifty percent since 1985, in fields such as math and statistics the numbers have hardly moved, from 15,009 college graduates in those fields in 1985 to 15,496 in 2009.[76] And in the fields of "microbiology, chemical engineering, and computer science, we graduated more students in those fields in 1985 than we do today."[77] Finally, more students graduate with college degrees in the visual and performing arts than in "computer science, math, and chemical engineering combined."[78] If paying off student debt, raising a family, or just supporting oneself is a concern of college students, this statistic should close the discussion: of the top twenty majors with the highest midcareer salaries, "all but one (economics) are STEM disciplines."[79] And I would include economics in the STEM category.

Let me provide some starker statistics to highlight the broken pipeline to the foregone possibilities, the missed American Dream if you will: Engineering degrees constitute about 4.7 percent of bachelors degrees awarded each year, and that is down from seven and eight percent in those fields two and three decades ago, which was already a pretty small percentage.[80] Computer science degrees constitute less than three percent of bachelors degrees, never having risen above five percent in the last forty years.[81] Biology?

3.7 percent.[82] Chemistry? Less than one percent.[83] Math? Just over one percent.[84] But the fields of psychology, art and performance, and education each routinely more than double the percentages of computer science degrees we award each year. We graduate four hundred percent more art and performance students from college each year than we do computer scientists—and five hundred percent more art and performance students than math students.

Meanwhile, a closer look at STEM readiness and preparedness in our students and workforce shows what it can mean for the country's growth as a whole.

The National Governors' Association report makes a point worth quoting at length:

> According to the Milken Institute's Best-Performing Cities 2010, "A rich innovation pipeline plays a pivotal role in a region's industrial development, commercialization, competitiveness, and ability to sustain long-term growth." The STEM workforce is a powerful component of this innovation pipeline. STEM occupations employ individuals who create ideas and applications that become commercialized and yield additional jobs. STEM fields overwhelmingly dominate other fields in generating new patents, including those that enter the marketplace. For example, during 1998–2003, scientists and engineers (S&E) applied for nearly 10 times more patents and commercialized almost eight times more patents than applicants from all other fields.
>
> STEM workers also contribute to the creation of innovation hubs—areas that usually include technology centers and research parks—that are important sources of economic activity. STEM workers are often found in high concentrations in these areas. In addition, research universities and other postsecondary institutions typically are nearby, providing new supplies of STEM graduates and opportunities for collaboration. Innovation hubs can spawn clusters of associated businesses and suppliers in both STEM and non-STEM fields while also rapidly growing jobs.[85]

And, as the U.S. Department of Commerce tells us, "The greatest advancements in our society from medicine to mechanics have come from the minds of those interested in or studied in the areas of STEM. Although still relatively small in number, the STEM workforce has an outsized impact on a nation's competitiveness, economic growth, and overall standard of living."[86]

What would raising our proficiency in math and science mean to the economy and growth of America? Various studies show a variety of results, but all reach the same conclusion: More growth. A lot more. According to a report by the National Governors' Association, the Council of Chief State School Officers, and Achieve, Inc., "If the United States raised students' math and science to globally competitive levels over the next two decades, its GDP would be an additional 36 percent higher 75 years from now."[87] More recently, McKinsey & Co. found that, "At the K–12 level, enhancing classroom instruction, turning around underperforming high schools, and introducing digital learning tools can boost student achievement. These initiatives could raise GDP by as much as $265 billion by 2020—and achieve a dramatic "liftoff" effect by 2030, adding as much as $1.7 trillion to annual GDP." That is greater than our current national budget deficit. Add the concept of reforming our teacher workforce by just five to seven percent, and we have not only erased our budgetary concerns, we will put America back into budget surpluses.

I know the excuses – students in the United States are more creative, better problem-solvers than students from other nations who excel in rote learning and test-taking. So in 2012, PISA tested problem-solving for the first time. How did we do? We scored about average, still behind Korea, China, and other nations. Then there is the excuse that other countries are vastly different than ours, culturally and in a great many other ways. So, compare Canada. As Standford's Eric Hanushek, Harvard's Paul Peterson, and University of Munich's Ludger Woessmann recently pointed out in their book *Endangering Prosperity*, while the United

States falls below most industrialized countries in international comparisons of mathematics achievement and proficiency of its 15-year-olds, it is beaten handily by Canada which is ranked 10th in the world (the United States is ranked 32nd). But Canada is not that culturally different from the United States: "the two countries share a common language, a common heritage, and a common border."[88] As Hanushek points out elsewhere, "Canada also has an influx of immigrants; they have strong unions; it's a federalist system."[89] But look at what it would mean for our economy if we could simply achieve what Canada achieves in its level of educational performance by 2025, giving us a little more than a decade to get there: "The average annual income of every worker in the United States over the next 80 years would be 20 percent higher....the gains from a faster-growing economy over the lifetime of somebody born today would amount to five times our current GDP [some $77 trillion]...enough to resolve the projected U.S. debt crisis."[90]

Let me explain some of this from a personal standpoint. I'm often asked why science, technology, engineering and math are the only words used to create the acronym, and when Project Lead The Way (PLTW), the STEM organization I am proud to lead, will change STEM to STEAM, STREAM or STEMM—incorporating art, reading or music into the acronym. This misses the fundamental point. Our societal, economic, and education problems are not anywhere near or about adding to acronyms, but instead adding to the relevancy of learning. Our solutions are about showing students how technical concepts relate to real-world situations and providing them with hands-on projects and problems that help them apply concepts in ever-new and changing contexts. It's about nurturing students' curiosity and helping them develop creativity, problem solving, critical thinking, and collaboration skills. STEM isn't simply the subjects in the acronym. It's an engaging and exciting way of teaching and learning. Or should be. And can be.

On a recent flight to a speaking engagement in California, I had a conversation with the person sitting next to me. She asked me what I did, and when I told her, she remarked, "Oh, you're one of those." When I asked what she did, she explained that she was the creative director for an advertising agency, and the world of STEM seems to disregard, even dismiss, the arts. Moments later, she began working on her MacBook Pro, loaded with state-of-the-art software. So my question to her was "Who do you think made that laptop and developed the software for artists and creators like you?" STEM fields are at the core of everything we do. STEM connects to everything, whether it is the arts, music, sports or agriculture.

Look no further than the materials and technology artists use: computers and graphics, paint, a canvas. Computer scientists develop the graphics technology, chemists work to ensure the right chemical composition to create vibrant colors, and engineers design a stronger canvas that absorbs the right amount of paint. Furthermore, the same creativity that inspires beautiful works of art is the same creativity that has led to some of the world's highest-performing, usable and visually appealing inventions. For instance, the Corvette Stingray, the 2014 North American Car of the Year, is an engineering marvel and one of the top-performing automobiles on the market. But, it's also aesthetically appealing. The same could be said for your new lightweight running shoes, your single-serving coffee maker, or the acoustically designed facilities for your community's symphony orchestra. These are all examples of engineering and the arts working together, and they all resulted from the same design process engineers use to build the world's most advanced fighter jets, develop new energy solutions, and create targeted therapies for chronic diseases.

STEM can be found in virtually every discipline and in every product. STEM is not exclusive to the subjects of science, technology, engineering, or math. We must continue engaging students in the STEM disciplines and encouraging them to combine technical knowledge and skills with the creativity that leads to innovative ideas—ideas that give the arts new technologies, music new instruments, farmers new machines, and our businesses a competitive advantage. Unless we continue building the STEM pipeline, each profession suffers. We end up encouraging the end product of art and performance while discouraging or neglecting science, technology, engineering, and math.

That is why education reform generally, and STEM education specifically, are the keys to our economic well-being and future.

3

Why We Fail & How To Fix It

It has been a full generation—thirty years—since the landmark "Nation at Risk" report was issued by the U.S. Department of Education. That report opened with this ominous warning: "Our Nation is at risk. Our once unchallenged preeminence in commerce, industry, science, and technological innovation is being overtaken by competitors throughout the world."[91] To add to the drama of the problem, the report's authors continued:

> If an unfriendly foreign power had attempted to impose on America the mediocre educational performance that exists today, we might well have viewed it as an act of war. As it stands, we have allowed this to happen to ourselves. We have even squandered the gains in student achievement made in the wake of the Sputnik challenge. Moreover, we have dismantled essential support systems which helped make those gains possible. We have, in effect, been committing an act of unthinking, unilateral educational disarmament.[92]

Since then, there have been any number of citations to the Nation at Risk, there have been any number of education reform proposals, we have overhauled testing regimens, and added billions of dollars into our education system. But the results over the past thirty years have been flat at best, with no appreciable change upward in our scores. I say "at best," because in many ways we have done worse. This chart of national expenditures and scores from 1970 to 2010 explains just about the whole story:

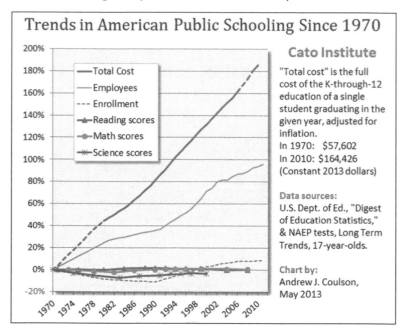

Trends in American Public Schooling Since 1970

Legend:
— Total Cost
— Employees
--- Enrollment
▲ Reading scores
● Math scores
✕ Science scores

Cato Institute

"Total cost" is the full cost of the K-through-12 education of a single student graduating in the given year, adjusted for inflation.
In 1970: $57,602
In 2010: $164,426
(Constant 2013 dollars)

Data sources:
U.S. Dept. of Ed., "Digest of Education Statistics," & NAEP tests, Long Term Trends, 17-year-olds.

Chart by:
Andrew J. Coulson,
May 2013

Spending went up, educational hires from teachers to administrators increased, and scores have flat-lined. The point is, we still do not get it right in American education: not in reading, not in writing, and not in the STEM fields. And, as stated earlier, we are spending more than other countries that do get it right. What is the problem? And why is it so hard to see and overcome?

The answers to these questions are partly pedagogical and partly cultural. Let me start with the pedagogical. In looking at the other countries whose students continually outmatch our students in the STEM fields, there is the answer of time. Other nations, especially the ones that beat us, simply put their students through more schooling. As education reform expert Chester E. Finn, Jr. put it recently:

Schoolchildren in China attend school 41 days a year more than most young Americans—and receive 30% more hours of instruction. Schools in Singapore operate 40 weeks a year. Saturday classes are the norm in Korea and other Asian countries—and Japanese authorities are having second thoughts about their 1998 decision to cease Saturday-morning instruction. This additional time spent learning is one big reason that youngsters from many Asian nations routinely out-score their American counterparts on international tests of science and math.[93]

Our students' "summer learning loss" is "no joke," Finn writes, as our students lose "a full month's worth [over the summer], by most estimates, adding up to 1.3 school years by the end of high school."[94] And then there is this: "students in other postindustrial countries receive twice as much instruction in core academic areas during high school."[95]

Take the issue of summer recess/break and summer learning for a moment. At a time when there is so much focus on American students' global education competitiveness, students and teachers at all grade levels should find opportunities to keep their minds active and continue learning while enjoying our vaunted and nearly-sacrosanct summer breaks. I am not against them, not at all. Our teachers need them, our principals need them, our parents and children need them.

But, still, summer learning loss is real. It is also counterproductive, requiring teachers to spend considerable time at the beginning of the new school year reviewing before they introduce new material and help students develop new and advanced skills. The National Summer Learning Association reports that students lose an equivalent of two months of their grade-level math computational skills over the summer, and students from low-income families also lose the same equivalency in reading achievement. While summer is a time to relax, it is not a time to stop learning.

The key to education—especially in critical STEM fields—is activity-based learning that makes concepts relevant in real-world, meaningful ways. In Project Lead The Way classroom curriculum, for example, velocity, speed, lift, and drag—concepts often taught in a high school physics class—are applied when building an airfoil that must meet certain constraints. In third grade, students learn about forces, axels and levers, and apply these concepts to design a simple machine to rescue an animal that has fallen into a trench. Lessons like these show students the relevancy of their learning and engage and inspire them to continue learning. But learning like this doesn't have to be confined to a classroom. Nor should it all be lost over the course of two and a half to three months.

While traditional summer school is beneficial for some students, summer learning does not have to mean spending all day inside a classroom or library. Summer activities are rife with real-world learning experiences that parents and communities can help convey: A swimming pool can teach students about buoyancy. The ocean waves can be a lesson in gravitational forces. A baseball game can teach about velocity and drag. Parents and children who enjoy baking together can turn the measurements into a math lesson on fractions. There are websites and apps, sites like Kahn Academy and PBS' Design Squad, that provide engaging lessons and activities for kids. Many tools can be accessed at a community library if a computer is not available in the home. Parents can also take time to encourage their child to read, helping build not only reading comprehension and vocabulary skills, but also knowledge on topics that students find interesting.

Summer camps are another great way to continue student learning. Organizations like Boy Scouts, Girl Scouts, Boys and Girls Clubs of America, 4H, and local zoos or museums offer exciting and engaging opportunities for students. Project Lead The Way partners with the Society of Manufacturing Engineers Education Foundation to support Gateway Academy camps across the United States. This past summer, nearly 5,000 middle school students spent a week immersed in hands-on activities building knowledge on topics like programming, alternative energy, flight and space, fluid power, and the engineering design process.

Summer is also a terrific time for teachers to improve their craft by engaging in professional development—not the kind of professional development that teaches the latest fads in education, but rather the kind that focuses on how teachers can engage students in relevant learning. Continuous teacher training and learning is vital to student success. A number of universities offer formal summer courses. Nonprofit organizations like Project Lead The Way offer rigorous, in-depth resident training programs. And while Massive Open Online Courses (MOOCs) have their supporters and opponents, a MOOC could be a great option for continuous teacher learning over the summer months.

Learning does not have to cease for the summer when the last class bell rings. Students, teachers and parents can have an enjoyable and relaxing summer, all while continuing the education process. The responsibility to continue learning during the summer rests with each one of us. When it comes to summer learning loss, we can change course. We can continuously improve, learn and engage, and have a great summer in the process.

We also must address the growing concern—more and more appreciated over the past few years—emphasizing teacher quality and compensation. As Michael Milken put it:

> Once upon a time, U.S. college graduates near the top of their classes routinely entered the teaching profession. In fact, 90 percent of new American teachers in the early to mid-20th century came from the upper third of their classes. Today, it's just 23 percent. Meanwhile, virtually 100 percent of teachers in Singapore, South Korea and Finland come from the top third of their graduating classes.[96]

And we now know that teacher quality is, after parent involvement, the single greatest factor in a child's education. As Microsoft Founder Bill Gates has said, "the single most decisive factor in student achievement is excellent teaching. It is astonishing what great teachers can do for their students."[97] William Bennett cites two graphic studies that tell the whole tale:

> [I]f you take an 8-year-old student performing at the 50th percentile and give him a low-performing teacher, he will regress to the 37th percentile in three years. Give him a high-performing teacher, and he will succeed to the 90th percentile in the same amount of time—a swing of 53 percentage points.[98]

And,

> According to an analysis by Stanford economist Eric Hanushek, if you replaced the lowest-performing teachers in our country (roughly 5% to 10% of the teaching work force) with just average performing teachers, America's students as a whole would rise from the bottom of the performance ladder on international tests to a Top 10 ranking. What would this mean for our GDP, by the way? Tens of trillions of dollars.[99]

A recent McKinsey study backs up an important element of this as well: the professionalism and skills of our teacher workforce. Comparing us to countries like Finland, Singapore, and South Korea—countries that continually beat us—McKinsey has found: "The U.S. does not take a strategic or systematic approach to nurturing teaching talent. Buffeted by a chaotic mix of labor market trends, university economics, and local school district and budget dynamics, we have failed to attract, develop, reward or retain outstanding professional teaching talent on a consistent basis."[100] Those countries, "recruit, develop and retain...'top third' students as one of their central education strategies, and they've achieved extraordinary results. These systems recruit 100% of their teacher corps from the top third of the academic cohort, and then screen for other important qualities as well. In the U.S., by contrast, 23% of new teachers come from the top third and just 14% in high poverty schools."[101]

Can we pay our good teachers more? Can we, once again, recruit from the top talent pool of college graduates to encourage and inspire entry into the teacher profession? Yes, we must—outside of the homeschooling community, we give our children to our nation's teachers for large parts of nearly every weekday and we invest in our teachers a similar trust to take care of our children. Teachers should be treated as professionals, respected as such, and rewarded as such. Many teachers I know deserve and get that respect, but they do not get the reward. I can think of no greater priority for our country than to turn around the national, cultural, and economical view of what good and great teachers should be paid—not only presently but for purposes of recruitment into the field.

What would recruiting more good and great teachers cost us? Let me be clear: it would be a net gain to our state budgets and economy. As the McKinsey study found, if you took a large school district with half of its schools serving a high poverty population, to attract and then double the portion of "top third" new hires in the teaching profession, it would cost half of one percent of the state's current K-12 spending.[102] If you took the nation's lowest-performing schools and applied the same recommended scenario "teachers would not pay for their initial training; high-needs schools would have effective principals and offer ongoing training comparable to the best professional institutions; districts would improve shabby and sometimes unsafe working conditions; the highest-performing teachers would receive performance bonuses of 20%; and the district or state would benefit from a marketing campaign promoting teaching as a profession," it would cost even less, two-tenths of one percent of K-12 spending.[103]

And, as we have seen from programs like Teach for America, at least in the short term, top college students, with ongoing professional training, respect, and a clear mission, even with entry-level teaching salaries, can be recruited to go into our nation's highest poverty schools. In fact, Teach for America rejects about 85 percent of its applicants.[104]

Compensation reform is not, of course, the panacea for teachers and satisfaction in their profession. As the annual MetLife survey of our nation's teachers' concerns shows, pay and salary are certainly important, but, as we know, most teachers do not go into the profession thinking about getting wealthy. Of equal or more importance to our nations' teachers are factors such as "opportunities for professional development," "time to collaborate with other teachers," "reduction in resources," and "concerns about job security."[105] I will talk more about this later with regard to PLTW's practice and experience in these factors. In sum, they are critical.

Still, there can be no question: if we want a teaching workforce that is regarded as professional, we must commit to improving compensation—not only to retain our best but to recruit our best. And while most teachers today are highly committed to their profession, there is—as with any profession—a stratum of ineffective teachers that must be removed from the classroom. The net cost and pay off? As Erik Hanushek of Stanford has found, a replacement of just five to seven percent of our least effective teachers could yield a net result of "an increase in total U.S. economic output of $112 trillion in present value."[106] As Dr. Hanushek points out in his research, and, I think bears repeating, $112 trillion is not a typo.

At the same time, not all of our problems are in the classroom. There is a cultural and familial dimension as well. Our national household spending priorities simply do not match the countries we are up against. As Michael Milken has pointed out, using Bureau of Labor Statistics numbers, the average Asian family spends about 15 percent of its disposable income on education while the average American family spends just two percent.[107] We beat Asia in disposable income spending on other things, of course, like transportation, entertainment, and housing—we tend to spend more on those, but not education. As Thomas Friedman once put it: "In China, Bill Gates is Britney Spears, in America Britney Spears is Britney Spears."[108] The point is, we get what we honor and esteem, and in Asia education is simply more honored and esteemed than in America.

And, of course, difficult family structures in America do not help. In fact, they not only compete with what we increasingly expect of teachers in the classroom but reams of social science research back up the predictability of educational attainment based on those structures. One study put it this way: "Compared with peers in intact families, children in single-parent families, stepparent families, or non-parent guardian families scored, on average, lower on math and science achievement tests, according to a large international survey. Family resources (e.g., number of books in the home, number of possessions, immigrant status, and household size) only partially explained the relationship between family structure and math and science achievement."[109] If the teacher is the second greatest influence on a child's learning, second to a parent, it only makes sense that children with both parents at home, engaged in their children's learning, will make a dramatic difference compared to children without those advantages and support structures.

Unfortunately, we cannot easily or immediately change family structure or several other cultural factors that lead to our STEM and other educational challenges. But we can change our national educational priorities, thinking, and structures. And, we can trade in what does not work for what does. What does not work? Let us start with persistence of students in STEM majors in U.S. colleges and universities. Recall that shrinking number of students that do go on to STEM-related coursework at the post-secondary level, that enter STEM-related fields of study as college freshman? Some forty to sixty percent of those students transition to other fields in what has been called the "math-science death march;" and, yes, this even takes place at some of our nation's most selective colleges and universities.[110]

The reasons for the "death march" are many, starting with students' lack of preparation and ability. Other experts—and students—report on the dry nature of the field of study while still others point to the comparative ease in the liberal arts and humanities: "the proliferation of grade inflation in the humanities and social sciences, which provides another incentive for students to leave STEM majors. It is no surprise that grades are lower in math and science, where the answers are clear-cut and there are no bonus points for flair,"[111] is how one education reporter puts it. One student profiled recently had an 800 score on the math portion of his SAT and over 700 on the reading and writing portions. He was heavily recruited in engineering. By his sophomore year he left the field: "I was trying to memorize equations, and engineering's all about the application, which they really didn't teach too well… It was just like, 'Do these practice problems, and then you're on your own.'"[112] A fan of poetry and of a psychology course he took his freshman year, he switched to a double major in psychology and English. Those classes, he said, "were a lot more discussion based."[113]

I see this phenomenon repeatedly. Part of the problem is grade inflation and the relative ease of the soft or softer sciences. And a large part of the problem is the dryness of the coursework—not enough design and interactive projects and simulations. But another large part of the problem was captured well by a psychology professor, Steven Pinker at Harvard—pointing to the lack of interdisciplinary connectedness between the sciences and liberal arts. "The great thinkers of the age of reason and the Enlightenment were scientists," Pinker writes, pointing to such intellectual giants as Descartes, Spinoza, Hobbes, Locke, Rousseau, and others:[114]

> Not only did many of them contribute to mathematics, physics, and physiology, but all of them were avid theorists in the sciences of human nature. They were cognitive neuroscientists, who tried to explain thought and emotion in terms of physical mechanisms of the nervous system. They were evolutionary psychologists, who speculated on life in a state of nature and on animal instincts that

are "infused into our bosoms." And they were social psychologists, who wrote of the moral sentiments that draw us together, the selfish passions that inflame us, and the foibles of shortsightedness that frustrate our best-laid plans.[115]

Today, we have scientific knowledge those giants "never dreamed of," so you would think, Pinker argues, scholars in the humanities and liberal arts would avail themselves of more of the ideas from the sciences. But, while "everyone endorses science when it can cure disease, monitor the environment, or bash political opponents, the intrusion of science into the territories of the humanities has been deeply resented." This has led to the creation of intellectual and academic silos at both our college and university levels and even in our elementary and secondary education teaching and thinking—more on that shortly. Think again about what uniting the fields, or interdisciplinary efforts could do for advances in both the sciences and liberal arts—after all, "A consilience with science offers the humanities countless possibilities for innovation in understanding. Art, culture, and society are products of human brains." [116] Pinker offers examples at the end of his essay:

> The humanities would enjoy more of the explanatory depth of the sciences, to say nothing of the kind of a progressive agenda that appeals to deans and donors. The sciences could challenge their theories with the natural experiments and ecologically valid phenomena that have been so richly characterized by humanists.

> In some disciplines, this consilience is a fait accompli. Archeology has grown from a branch of art history to a high-tech science. Linguistics and the philosophy of mind shade into cognitive science and neuroscience.

> Similar opportunities are there for the exploring. The visual arts could avail themselves of the explosion of knowledge

in vision science, including the perception of color, shape, texture, and lighting, and the evolutionary aesthetics of faces and landscapes. Music scholars have much to discuss with the scientists who study the perception of speech and the brain's analysis of the auditory world.

And there is much to say about what science can do with and for political science and literature as well (and Pinker does). The point flows in both directions: science classes would not only benefit from more understandings from the liberal arts but the "math-science death march" could be slowed by such importations. If science or engineering students see their courses as dull compared to what is being taught in, say, the psychology classrooms and labs, all would benefit from more of an interdisciplinary curricula, beginning with interaction with faculty from other fields in each other's classrooms and labs, when and where the opportunity for connections and mutual learning and benefits can be shown.

This is one way to think about saving not only the humanities but also inspiring and keeping students in the math and science disciplines. No field should be isolated, on an island, or in a silo... the great minds of the Enlightenment, for one, did not see their studies that way, they saw unifying themes and an intellectual relationship between all their theories and works. This issue gets us to the elementary and secondary education levels as well.

In his five reforms suggested to reinvigorate STEM education in K-12 education, two of Secretary of Education William Bennett's suggestions to education reformers are indeed along these lines:

> Do not segregate math and science classes from the rest of the school building or coursework. Turn away from the notion of specialized elementary and secondary schools whose focus is on math and science. These areas of study should be in all schools and deemed a critical part of each and every school's broad curriculum. Students who excel in these areas should not be seen as "different" or labeled as "special" or worse.

Each and every class taught, where possible and relevant, should adopt forms of mathematical and scientific methods in its pedagogy, engage in practices of "building models, arguing from evidence and communicating findings" so as to "increase the likelihood that students will learns the ideas of science or engineering and mathematics at a deeper, more enduring level," as two STEM scholars recently suggested.[117]

As I move into other reforms for K-12 education, let me summarize Dr. Bennett's other suggestions as well: front-load STEM-related teaching. We should seek out children's natural intellectual curiosities and teach mathematical and scientific concepts earlier in school, treating those subjects as important as reading and writing. Front-loading STEM concepts is critical and preschool is not too early to start. We must also do a better job of training teachers, especially in the early grades, in math and science so that they can integrate those subjects and topics as much as possible into their curricula. Finally, schools should avail themselves of non-profit organizations like Project Lead The Way, organizations with records of success in teacher training and student success.[118]

Simply put, one can read all the academic papers and studies one wants, there are reams, and I have reviewed most of them. But they all conclude that we have at least five problems we need to overcome: Engaging students in STEM subjects too late and then not enough; teaching poor and boring content; not integrating math and science with other subjects; ineffective teacher training; and a paucity of women and minorities in the fields.

Working backwards, the issue of inspiring more women and minorities in the STEM related fields is one I take personally, not only because I know these fields to be promising economically but also because I know it can be done. Take Toppenish High School in the State of Washington, about which I will have more to say later: Toppenish has a student population of over ninety percent minority and nearly all of the students come from low-income families. Nevertheless, their former principal, Trevor Greene, instituted Project Lead The Way's rigorous engineering and biomedical sciences program for which he credits much of his school's success. From starting with a handful of engineering classes at the high school level, today there are over thirty sections of PLTW classes at Toppenish.

At the college level, Freeman Hrabowski—whose life story in civil rights began at the age of twelve when he marched with Martin Luther King, Jr. and who is now the President of the University of Maryland at Baltimore County (UMBC—a PLTW Affiliate University)—has spoken about how UMBC has successfully changed the prospects of so many underrepresented minorities in the STEM fields.[119] President Hrabowski outlines what he calls the "Four Pillars" of college success in science, four things that helped to make UMBC such a success in graduating students in STEM fields, especially among minority populations. The first pillar is encouraging high expectations, hard work, and attendance. Many students fail, drop out, or simply score low in their first-year college science course. That is why those courses are often known as or called "weed out" courses. Encourage students to retake those courses just as many political science students have to retake economic and statistics courses.

Note, too, that not missing school, not missing classes, is a huge predictor of success just as study after study is now showing that absenteeism is a predictor of failure and dropping out. (One recent study revealed a "miss one/lose one" relationship where each day of missed school translated to scoring a point lower on high stakes tests).[120] The second pillar is building community among students—encouraging the more advanced and successful students to mentor and tutor the less initially successful students. Getting rid of the cut-throat idea of learning and making it more of a group effort among students matters. The third pillar encourages researchers to produce researchers. The importance of labs cannot be overstated, true research is about life to students, not just school for school's sake. Finally, the fourth pillar is interested faculty: a connection between teachers and students where the teachers take personal or individual interest in students who are falling behind.

At the national level, organizations such as the National Action Council for Minorities in Engineering (NACME) are confronting this issue. Under the leadership of Dr. Irving McPhail, NACME is advancing its mission to increase the number of successful underrepresented minorities in STEM careers. Through programs such as college scholarships and Engineering Academies in partnership with PLTW and the National Academies Foundation, NACME is committed to improving America's human capital and global competitiveness.

Turning to women in STEM fields, I have seen programs like the Perry Initiative, dedicated to inspiring female students to go into the fields of orthopedics and engineering, change students' minds and lives. The Perry Initiative, with the leadership of co-founder Dr. Jenni Buckley, does it the way PLTW does it: with inspiring role models and hands-on experience. As an example— two dozen female students from a high school science class take their Saturday to go to a Mayo Clinic for an all-day, hands-on, instruction on orthopedics led by female orthopedic surgeons, students working with the actual tools of the trade, including students putting stitches into flesh (cow tongues in most cases).

The need here is great. Women are about half the workforce in America but hold less than a quarter of STEM-related jobs. As for minorities, they receive less than 15 percent of our nation's bachelor's degrees in science.[121] Part of the answer to inspiring more minorities and women in the STEM fields is the same as inspiring other students—starting earlier, with engaging teachers and role models, and recruitment and encouragement from teachers, parents, principals, and coaches. As an educator, I know the importance of eliminating pernicious stereotypes that elevate some students and stifle others. The National Alliance for

Partnerships in Equity is doing excellent work here, and I especially like what Mimi Lufkin, the group's CEO, says about mentoring:

> Women leaders in positions of influence must bring their valuable perspective and experience to the table and support the advancement of other women in STEM. Leadership is using your position of power and influence to help create a culture of inclusion for everyone in STEM such as: mentoring other women to take on leadership opportunities; removing barriers for those coming after you; standing up, speaking up and solving inequities in your sphere of influence; balancing work and family through example and by supporting family friendly workplace policies; and by being a role model for the men and women who work with you and for the young women in your community.

As for starting earlier, I cannot emphasize this enough. Young minds form academic attitudes and prejudices early. Turn a student off from math or science in an early grade and you can almost never make up for that. Turn a student on in an early grade, and the possibilities are endless. In fact, one recent study of science graduate students and professionals found that over forty percent of them reported first becoming interested in their fields between kindergarten and fifth grade.[122] Another study of 5,000 science students, tracking them through college, found that "positive classroom experiences, such as relating the content to students' lives, were strongly associated with the completion of a college degree in STEM."[123]

We are not doing a good job of encouraging this now. According to a recent study commissioned by Intel, today, sixty-three percent of teenagers never consider a profession in engineering, nearly thirty percent of teenagers do not know of any potential jobs in engineering, and twenty percent cannot explain anything about engineering's impact on the world.[124] But, supporting what I said above, the same study found that "exposure to any facts about engineering leads more than half of teens to say they are more likely to consider engineering as a career." Simply talking about engineering, explaining what it does and is, and what fields it opens the doors to, changes half of teens' minds! The study's recommendations on how to accomplish this are:

> Focus on helping teens understand what being an engineer is all about. Improving understanding of what engineers actually do can increase consideration, so talk about how rewarding it is to be an engineer.
>
> Don't dumb down what engineers do. Try to reframe the difficulty of engineering as a positive challenge, a badge of honor to be worn proudly when successful.
>
> Make engineering feel less remote and more personal. Give a face to engineers to help inspire and create a sense that "if they can do it, I can do it."
>
> Up-weight the emotional appeal of engineering. The societal benefits of what engineers do, like preventing disasters or generating cleaner electricity, are particularly resonant with teens that have never considered engineering before.[125]

This really is not complicated, but it is intentional—teachers, parents, counselors, coaches, principals must show and express interest. And, since the private sector has a significant stake in student engagement and success, it must be involved with our schools. As David Steel, the Executive Vice President of Strategy for Samsung Electronics North America, points out, aside from sponsoring science fairs, and showing up at job fairs, employees from Boeing to Facebook to Apple and IBM (and from all the tech products elementary, middle, and high school students use) should make efforts—out of their own companies' future workforce and self-interest if nothing else—to get into classrooms. And principals and teachers should reach out to these companies to send them representatives. "Increased interaction between students and STEM professionals can help show that it is possible to study STEM subjects and still be cool," Steel writes.[126]

A great example of a company committed to getting into classrooms is Lockheed Martin. Recognizing the importance of role models for students, thousands of Lockheed Martin engineers participate in the company's Engineers in the Classroom program. Practicing professionals regularly collaborate with students on design projects, help students understand the importance of learning math and science, and inform students about the tremendous career opportunities available to them.

Over the years, Lockheed Martin has provided financial support to dozens of schools to help implement PLTW programs. Given the programs' success, the company recently announced a multi-year, multi-million dollar investment to implement PLTW K-12 programs in several of America's largest urban school districts.

Then, beyond the doing of STEM, in class and in work, there is the importance of highlighting and encouraging teachers and students. One idea a colleague of mine deployed in his home-state of Arizona was to put STEM teachers and their science fair students on his radio show—showing the rest of the city what great teachers and students can do and are doing, and making the experience for the teacher and the student all the more interesting and "cool" along the way. Radio listeners love education as a topic. "Think about it," he says, "Everyone has some experience in education, having been a student, a parent, a teacher, you name it. A little secret about radio I did not know going in was that if you want calls and opinions and interest, make education the issue." Principals: contact your local radio show hosts and tell them about your excelling STEM teachers and students…and try and get them on the air.

Of course, having the right teachers in America's classrooms is where this all starts. Here are just two statistics highlighting the problem: Right now, one third of public middle school science teachers and thirty-six percent of public middle school math teachers either did not major in those subjects in college and/

or are not certified to teach them.[127] Meanwhile, too many states and school districts do not allow for the kinds of alternative certifications that interested prospective teachers could obtain without going through a traditional certification route. Put simply, it is difficult to transmit a love of a topic, never mind the basics of it, when one is not trained in it. I wrote above about how we need to, and can, recruit teachers from the tops of their classes. It's not such a tall order; Teach for America does this every year, and selects a small cohort from a large pool of highly talented graduates from America's leading colleges and universities. But we also need to re-engage a civil and national conversation about teacher certification, merit pay, time off for additional training, more attractive salaries in underperforming schools, and metrics regarding licensure and even dismissal. This is not a conservative/ liberal debate or a right/left argument. While many education experts in the field who have been arguing for these reforms tend to come from what are known as "conservative" think tanks, such reforms are also supported by non-ideological organizations like the Bill and Melinda Gates Foundation, Democrats like Michelle Rhee, and in fact, one of the most prominent liberal think tanks, the Center for American Progress, has issued a paper advocating just these things.[128]

The research on inspiring teachers, excellent teachers, in their fields is conclusive and really cannot be controversial anymore. We can debate how to do it, but look at what just one recent study from two economists from Harvard and Columbia found when they studied the Value Added approach to teacher quality (Value Added is a tool to measure performance based on students' test score increases, or decreases): "[R]eplacing a teacher whose true value-added is in the bottom 5% with a teacher of average quality would generate lifetime earnings gains worth more than $250,000 for the average classroom. On the other hand, 'If you leave a low value-added teacher in your school for 10 years, rather than replacing him with an average teacher, you are hypothetically talking about

$2.5 million in lost income."[129] Again, great teachers make all the difference; even average teachers make great differences. It's the bottom, small minority—roughly five percent—of the workforce that causes most of our concerns.

So, what can be done? The good news, and the reason I am optimistic, is that we have great STEM programs working in schools across America—and, an abundance of knowledge and research available to each of us not just in books or university libraries or studies presented at conferences, but through MOOCs and other online resources. One can go to the websites of Change the Equation or Project Lead The Way to access any number of studies and articles substantiating all I have written here. STEMConnector. org also hosts a set of great resources, including profiles of success stories and a daily, emailed, newsletter on the latest in STEM-related news. And one can take any of the foregoing knowledge to school principals and PTAs and curriculum committees to demand more and better STEM programming in your children's schools.

Of course, too, not all of this starts at the school level. I urge every parent to take time with his and her children to talk about the great discoveries and discoverers and scientists and inventors of our time. One can do this with biographies of everyone from the Wright Brothers to Sally Ride, from Thomas Edison to Steve Jobs. What did they learn? How did they learn it? How did they fail and try again? What effect did those people have on society? These are great conversations to have with children. And for children struggling in math and science classes, or who need extra help, sit with your child through Internet-based classes and tutorials, of which there are a growing number, including, most notably, the Khan Academy.

Engage your children civically and ask community leaders to sponsor a science and jobs opportunity fair. Congressman Frank Wolf of Virginia does this regularly, bringing in local and regional STEM-oriented professionals to highlight their work and meet with middle school and high school students. Every congressional district in America should be doing the same. This is a winning approach for everyone: it is in the schools' interests, it is in the local employers' interests, and involving elected officials with either his or her schools and local corporations is in their interest.

Talk with your school's principal to ensure highly effective and proven STEM programs, such as Project Lead The Way or the Perry Initiative, are available to your children. In sum, do everything you can to engage your child's interest and support it at the school.

Now let's address the question of education reform more generally. To systemically improve overall student achievement, we must have a concerted effort that includes a variety of reforms such as longer school days, more instructional days in the school year, high-quality early childhood education programs for all children, rewarding successful teachers, paying high-performing teachers more in salaries and bonuses, and changing the pedagogical approach in K-12 and post-secondary education. Fortunately, there is already some good news to report even here.

There are opportunities, for example, to get involved in the way we go about teaching math and science with the new Next Generation Science Standards and the Common Core State Standards which are being implemented in the vast majority of states. There has been some controversy over the Common Core but the fact is they are being deployed—so the question is not so much what is in them now as it is how they will be used. Indeed, one of the positive aspects of the standards is that they allow school districts and teachers to determine how they will be taught. Get involved now—it is a perfect opportunity that we must not miss.

Despite the political arguments around the idea of the Common Core, it is important to keep in mind that it represents standards, not curriculum. Our students are educated in local schools, but they will compete for jobs across the country and around the globe. Kirsten Baesler, North Dakota's superintendent of public instruction, made one of the most compelling arguments for the Common Core at a recent meeting I participated in with the Council of Chief State School Officers. She described a family that had recently moved to her state from Arizona. The children were highly successful by all measures, including doing very well on Arizona's state assessments. But when the student's results came back from the North Dakota state exams, their performance was significantly below expectations. Deeply concerned about the students, Superintendent Baesler—the students' vice principal at the time—began comparing North Dakota and Arizona state standards to discover significant differences, not in the quality of the standards, but of the grade level in which certain concepts were introduced. The students were learning, but they had simply not been introduced to the material at the time they took the tests in North Dakota.

Then, she described a visit to a local school district where teachers and administrators were celebrating the return to school. In welcoming all the new students, teachers marched into the auditorium carrying flags representing the states from which the new students had come. There were 32 state flags. There are thousands of these situations every day throughout thousands of school across the United States. Students move from state to state, from district to district, from school to school. It just makes sense that we have common standards. Not having common standards perpetuates our national and international education deficits, and simply leaves our competitiveness to chance.

What we need are robust common standards by which we will evaluate all students' performance. If the standards are not high enough for your students, increase them. If you want to connect the standards and curriculum to local uniqueness, then do it. If you want to teach a certain way that is effective, that is the point. The College Board's Advanced Placement program is based on common frameworks with nationally standardized tests. We need this because students go to college and universities all over the country and we need a common way to evaluate student performance. The same is true for the SAT and ACT. It just makes sense. By way of one illustration absent a Common Core-type plan: Wisconsin, according to the Thomas B. Fordham Foundation, has such different (or lagging) standards from the rest of the country that their students could achieve proficiency in certain subjects while their scores were actually lower than seventy percent of the students from other states.[130]

Or, take Louisiana. As one former public school teacher, and now-professional math tutor and businessman there recently put it: he was stunned by a story a few years back about a high school valedictorian at one of New Orleans' high schools. This valedictorian could not pass the math portion of Graduate Exit Exam. Indeed, she failed it six times.[131] This story can be replicated and found throughout the country, where students are number one at their school, but underperform in basic subjects on a national or international scale—they get passed along and up, until it is often too late to teach them any more. Stories like these were why this teacher (now businessman) supported the Common Core in Louisiana. He also made a great point about the economy. Sure, offshore and Indian gaming casinos can be fun and can provide jobs. But how much better would the jobs and economy be with a Fortune 500 company not involved in the gaming industry be? To that end, he made the excellent point: "IBM just announced plans to open an 800-person software development center in Baton Rouge. Such a center can only be successful if IBM is able to hire employees whose math skills are on par with employees of Asian companies, and there's no doubt that IBM would have gone elsewhere if Louisiana had failed to adopt the more challenging Common Core standards for math."[132]

There is both a conservative and a liberal case to be made for the Common Core, which is to say it should not be a political issue—after all, how many things do former Governor Jeb Bush (Florida), Governor Jan Brewer (Arizona), former Governor Mike Huckabee (Arkansas) and President Barack Obama agree on? Charles Blow of *The New York Times* got it right, the time for bright and shiny new concepts, yet another deployed educational experiment that sets us all back or delays our progress, should be long past over. We actually do know what works: "[W]e need a national standard for what kind of education we want our children to receive. Our educational system has become so tangled in experiments and exams and excuses that we've drifted away from the basis of what makes education great: learning to think critically and solve problems."[133]

Katherine Porter-McGee and Sol Stern, nationally recognized education analysts who fall on the conservative ideological divide of the education reform movement—scholars from the Fordham and Manhattan Institutes, respectively—have written up their case for the Common Core this way:

> The Common Core standards are also not a curriculum; it's up to state and local leaders to choose aligned curricula. [Having] carefully examined the new expectations and compared them with existing state standards: [We] found that for most states, Common Core is a great improvement in rigor and cohesiveness.[134]

And when it comes to the controversial math standards and the Common Core, Porter-McGee and Stern, find this: "mathematical content dominates the [Common Core] K–12 expectations. Unlike many of the replaced state standards, Common Core demands automaticity (memorization) with basic math facts, mastery of standard algorithms, and understanding of critical arithmetic. These essential foundational math skills are not only required but prioritized, particularly in the early grades. The math standards focus in depth on fewer topics that coherently build over time."

In conclusion on the Common Core, let me put it this way: Yes, I agree, states should not be coerced into adopting the Common Core or any set of standardized lesson plan, instruction, or goal. States should be free, as the Common Core intended, to adopt them and use them at their will. Governor Brewer of Arizona, as conservative a governor as one can find, understood this and adopted the Core under a different name. Fine. But here's my challenge to those so opposed to something like a Common Core: If we got rid of it tomorrow, would students be better off? Would parents? Would there be less indoctrination (for those who are concerned, legitimately concerned) about that? Would scores be higher? Dropouts lower? Teacher quality better? Of course not— that is the system we have had for the past two generations that has failed us and led us to the very problems I detail here.

4

I Am Convinced We Can Do This

To be clear, there is no shortage of organizations trying to address the issues I have written about. Home-grown school programs have sprouted across the country, organizations have developed local or regional programs, and a few have aspired to implement programs on a national scale.

But scaling to a national level requires more than just good intentions. Many organizations underestimate the importance of robust data systems, partner networks, and generally lack the human and financial capital to create an infrastructure necessary to grow the organization. Then there is the essential question of program efficacy. Many organizations lack research and measurable student outcomes, and the systems to collect performance data. And even if a program achieves positive results in an isolated implementation, can those results be replicated without quality degradation on a national level?

Even with these issues addressed, fledgling organizations now face the significant challenge of sustainability, particularly as the philanthropic support gap widens within an organization and they are challenged to raise more capital to expand and sustain operations. This is at a time in which companies and foundations are embracing accountability, proven strategies, and making high value-add investments from which they expect a return.

Project Lead The Way has navigated these issues. That is why Change the Equation, a CEO-led organization, recently endorsed PLTW as one of only four STEM programs of high quality and ready to be taken to scale nationally; the Social Impact Exchange named PLTW to its S&I 100 Index of non-profit organizations providing widespread impact and great promise of scalability; and PLTW received the national CLASSY award for educational advancement. PLTW is the only STEM organization endorsed by the Aerospace Industries Association.

PLTW was the vision of teacher Richard Blais and began in 1997 in twelve high schools in upstate New York. The mission was to inspire students and address the shortage of engineering students at the college level. Mr. Blais earned the support of the Liebich Family, and their Charitable Leadership Foundation provided substantial support to develop and expand the program. Over the years, PLTW has enjoyed tremendous support from several companies and foundations. Most notably, in 2007, the Kern Family Foundation, believing in PLTW's potential to transform K-12 education and students' lives, began a multi-million-dollar strategic investment to help take PLTW to a national scale.

Now based in Indianapolis, Indiana, PLTW has nearly 8,000 programs operating in more than 6,500 schools serving hundreds of thousands of students in all fifty states and the District of Columbia. PLTW is growing rapidly because it is effective, and because of a vast network of business and philanthropic partners, excellent teachers, and college and university affiliates.

The need for highly effective, nationally scalable STEM solutions could not be greater. The Department of Commerce estimates that the number of STEM jobs will grow seventeen percent by 2018 versus 9.8 percent for all other fields. Employers, however, report they are unable to find the talent required to fill these STEM jobs, leaving the United States, by 2018, with more than 1.2 million unfilled STEM jobs. While this may sound like an outstanding opportunity for American students, it will mean nothing if we do not adequately prepare our students to fill these jobs.

America's STEM crisis must be addressed now. If we are to succeed as a nation, we must adequately prepare our students for success in post-secondary education and careers. PLTW's work is centered on building a pipeline of well-educated and well-trained STEM professionals ready to compete in a rapidly changing global economy.

So, what makes PLTW unique from science, technology, engineering, and math courses already taught in schools? Professor Howard Gardner of Harvard says the greatest deficit for American students is their inability to apply learning in a context in which it was not learned. In America, we teach subjects in isolation and tend to teach "a mile wide and an inch deep." This is where PLTW is different. PLTW students create, design, build, discover, collaborate, and solve problems while applying core concepts from math, science, and other academic areas. In other words, PLTW focuses on depth over breadth in an interdisciplinary approach to learning where core academic content is applied rather than taught in isolated subject areas. It is the difference between solving the Pythagorean theorem and designing a suspension bridge in 3D modeling software, followed by prototyping and testing to determine load bearing—it's the difference between dry and boring, and exciting and relevant. This hands-on, project- and activity-based approach appeals to diverse students and engages them on multiple levels, introduces them to areas of study that they typically do not pursue, and provides them with the foundation to continue on a proven path to college and career success. PLTW classrooms are innovation zones where rigorous academic standards are integrated and students collaborate to apply academic content in a real-world context.

Additionally, PLTW programs are successful in all school sizes and types, including public, private, public charter, parochial, urban, suburban, and rural schools—both small and large. On a consistent basis, PLTW's programs are positively impacting students and their ability to succeed in achieving their desired educational and career goals. In addition to academic skills, students learn 21st-century skills pertinent to becoming highly qualified professionals. Our students learn how to communicate effectively, work in teams, facilitate discussions, practice professional conduct, think critically, and problem-solve.

Take the story of Josh, a PLTW graduate from Francis Tuttle Technology Center in Oklahoma City. In a recent interview, Josh described his PLTW experience in engineering, which combined applied learning with rigorous math and science emphasis. He talked about how the program helped students develop their presentation and communication skills while solving meaningful problems. Josh's capstone project in Engineering Design and Development was driven by a problem he dealt with at work concerning shoe theft. Through his work at Kohl's Department Store, he collected actual data and enlisted the help of the store manager and security. Josh led a student team that designed a Radio Frequency Identification (RFID) inventory system with the help of professionals in the field and his own intense research. They prototyped the solution and presented their working solution to several other business CEOs. The summer after his senior year of high school, he completed an internship at Surgery Logistics, creating a connection between the company's vision for RFID and Near Field Communication (NFC) in the health care environment. Josh is now an engineering student at Oklahoma State University (a PLTW Affiliate). He has started his own company, RFID Edge, which promotes STEM education for the secondary education sector on RFID and NFC. He interned at the Riata Center for Entrepreneurship at OSU, served in the Freshman Research Program, on the Freshman Representative Council for the College of Engineering, and is a member of the Entrepreneurship Club.

While many STEM programs only focus on certain students,

PLTW aspires to prepare all students in grades K-12 at various learning levels. The PLTW model accommodates a range of implementations and provides flexibility at a local level. PLTW supports the U.S. workforce by engaging students, regardless of their backgrounds, in STEM disciplines and building a pipeline for future professionals.

Let's now return to Toppenish High School in rural Washington at the heart of the Yakima Nation. As the school's principal, Trevor Greene transformed the school culture into one of high expectations for all students. He expanded academic opportunities for his students, many of whom were not expected to graduate high school. Greene added rigorous courses, including more than thirty sections of PLTW Engineering and Biomedical Science courses. Greene also increased student interest and success in post-secondary education. Through PLTW and its affiliate universities, students have the opportunity to earn up to thirty hours of college credit by the time they graduate high school. He has also prioritized parental and community involvement, reaching out to migrant families and the Yakima Nation on the very reservation where he grew up. In 2013, Greene was named the MetLife/NASSP High School Principal of the Year, one of the highest honors given to secondary educators.

We also know that women comprise only fourteen percent of the engineering workforce. Schools like Hilliard Davidson High School near Columbus, Ohio, are great models for recruiting and inspiring more girls in engineering studies. After three years of teaching PLTW engineering courses, instructor Bill Kuch noticed a problem—out of the eighty students in his four engineering classes, only eight were female. "The girls who were in the classes were incredibly successful and were staying in the program," Kuch said. "So we started brainstorming and thought, 'What if we had an all-female Introduction to Engineering Design course?'" Kuch discovered The Ohio State University's (OSU) Women in Engineering (WiE) program that provides mentors to female engineering majors. He partnered with OSU's WiE program to create Hilliard Davidson's own Women in Engineering program, replicating some of OSU's female outreach efforts: inviting female engineers to speak to classes, serve as mentors to the students, and recruit girls to engineering before they enter high school. Hilliard Davidson High School has realized significant improvement in a short period.

One year after beginning the WiE course sections, their female enrollment increased from eight percent to twenty-six percent. In the first year, all female engineering students passed the rigorous End of Course Assessment, and they outperformed the boys! Hilliard Davidson High School's Women in Engineering program has also led to increased female retention in engineering courses as the girls progress through high school. Not only did more girls register for the freshman year course, all but two continued on to Principles of Engineering the following year—with the boys. Forty percent of Hilliard Davidson High School's freshman year engineering students are now females. During my visit to Hilliard Davidson, it was clear that the girls had developed confidence and were inspired to pursue STEM careers. Programs such as this build a pipeline of talented female engineering students for colleges, universities, and employers. The strategies used at Toppenish and Hilliard provide just two examples of how schools are addressing these issues.

Our work is urgent. That is why we are committed to making PLTW accessible to every student in the United States—in traditional and non-traditional school settings. We must recruit, encourage, and inspire more students through these studies, targeting all students in general and underrepresented minorities and girls specifically. Then we must work tirelessly to help prepare our students to compete in our evolving, complex global economy. PLTW does this through our three pillars, designed to change the student experience, teacher pedagogy, and the way schools and communities interact.

World-Class Curriculum

Project Lead The Way's® approach, using activity-, project-, and problem-based (APPB) learning, focuses on hands-on, real-world projects that help students understand how the information and skills they are learning in the classroom can be applied in everyday life. PLTW's programs are comprehensive and aligned to Common Core State Standards for Math and English, Next Generation Science Standards, and other national and state standards. Yet, the programs are flexible and customizable so that schools can meet their curricular and community needs.

PLTW's team of professional curriculum writers along with industry experts, college professors, current teachers, and educational leaders develop each program. Programs are then regularly evaluated and improved to align with academic standards, student needs, and market changes.

PLTW *Launch* is an engaging, module-based program for students in kindergarten through grade five. Since students often determine whether they are good at math and science at an early age, *Launch* is designed to demystify these subjects and to encourage a love of STEM. Students use the design process and learn to problem solve, think critically, and work collaboratively. They learn that discoveries come from taking risks, and trial and error. Throughout the program, teachers and students learn and discover together, creating a highly engaging learning environment.

The PLTW *Gateway* program features a project-based curriculum designed to challenge and engage the natural curiosity and imagination of middle school students. Students acquire knowledge and skills in problem solving, teamwork and innovation as well as explore STEM careers in nine-week units taught in conjunction with a rigorous academic curriculum. Students envision, design and test their ideas using industry-standard modeling software. They study mechanical and computer control systems with robotics and automation. Students also explore the importance of energy, including innovative ways to reduce, conserve and produce it using a variety of sources. The knowledge that students gain and the skills they build in Gateway create a strong foundation for further STEM learning in PLTW's high school programs.

PLTW *Engineering* is a high school program of study that complements traditional mathematics and science courses. Students learn and apply the design process, acquire a strong proficiency in teamwork and communication, and develop organizational, critical-thinking, and problem-solving skills. Students learn and apply the design process, acquire a strong proficiency in teamwork and communication, and develop organizational, critical-thinking, and problem-solving skills. Students use the same industry-leading 3-D design software from Autodesk used by companies like Lockheed Martin and Intel. They explore aerodynamics, astronautics, and space life sciences. Students apply biological and engineering concepts related to biomechanics. They build and program robots from Vex Robotics. They discover how things are made. They design, test, and construct circuits and devices such as smart phones and tablets and work collaboratively on a culminating capstone project.

PLTW *Biomedical Sciences* is a high school program of study in which students explore the concepts of human medicine and are introduced to topics such as physiology, genetics, microbiology and public health. Through engaging activities, students examine the processes, structures and interactions of the human body— often playing the role of biomedical professionals. Students also use case studies to explore the prevention, diagnosis and treatment of disease, working collaboratively to investigate and design innovative solutions to modern health challenges such as fighting cancer.

Former United States President Bill Clinton called PLTW's newest high school program, *Computer Science*, a "game changer." *Computer Science* will be a high school program of study focused on areas such as computational thinking, coding, data mining, and cyber security.

High-Quality Teacher Training

The exponential growth in our programs nationwide derives from the development of engaging and immersive curriculum that impacts the lives of students. PLTW provides the curriculum, but relies on the expertise of individual teachers to make the coursework interactive, engaging, innovative, and challenging. Thousands of teachers have trained in PLTW's three-phase teacher training program.

Readiness Training is delivered online and represents the first phase of the PLTW professional development program. It is focused on ensuring that participants have basic technical and content knowledge prior to participating in pedagogy, skill, and knowledge enhancement training experiences.

Core Training is the second phase of the PLTW professional development program. It is an intensive and immersive in-person training experience hosted by PLTW's Affiliate Universities. In 2014, over 6,000 teachers trained with more than 400 PLTW Master Teachers and Affiliate Professors—a cadre of America's best and brightest STEM educators. During Core Training, teachers are immersed in course-specific curriculum; assume the role of the student to directly inform their expertise in content instruction; complete hands-on activities, projects, and problems with a strong focus on pedagogy; and become active members within a professional learning community.

Ongoing Training is the third phase of the PLTW professional development program and is largely administered virtually through PLTW's Learning Management System. It is designed to provide PLTW teachers with opportunities for continuous professional development to further their understanding of course tools, content, and concepts after they have successfully completed Core Training.

PLTW teacher training is highly effective. It is exactly the kind of professional learning that teacher and professional peer engagement surveys show teachers want and are most successful with in transforming their practice and the student experience. And it is the type of experience that helps recruit the best teachers and keep them teaching.

Engaged Partners Network

In addition to world-class curriculum and high-quality teacher training, partnerships are critical to PLTW's success. No one person, school, district, state, or organization can do this work alone. With a focus on building the STEM pipeline, our partners provide advocacy, resources and equipment for schools, mentors and role models for students, and local relevance and guidance for teachers.

Central to PLTW's extensive network are Affiliate institutions. This impressive group includes more than forty institutions ranked by U.S. News and World Report as the nation's leading engineering and biomedical science schools such as the University of Illinois, Duke University, Purdue University, Rose-Hulman Institute of Technology, and the Milwaukee School of Engineering. Affiliate institutions provide outreach to K-12 schools, host PLTW's teacher training program, and conduct professional development conferences for school administrators and counselors.

For example, Missouri University of Science and Technology (Missouri S&T) has helped implement hundreds of PLTW programs throughout their state, provided substantial support and expertise to schools, and they actively recruited PLTW students to their university. At the 2013 PLTW Missouri State Conference —attended by 800 teachers, counselors, administrators, and community leaders—Chancellor Cheryl Schrader spoke about her university's commitment to PLTW and STEM Education, and Governor JayNixon commended Missouri S&T and committed his support to making PLTW available to all Missouri students. This is the type of engagement necessary to improve education in communities, regions, and states.

Because PLTW students are prepared for post-secondary education with essential problem-solving, critical-thinking, and collaboration skills, hundreds of colleges and universities recruit and provide additional recognition opportunities for PLTW students with preferential admission, scholarships, and college credit. For instance, the University of South Carolina reported that sixty percent of its 2013-14 freshman engineering students are PLTW alumni, and the University of Minnesota and Milwaukee School of Engineering both reported nearly forty percent.

PLTW has also developed partnerships with organizations focused on enhancing the student experience, such as the College Board, NAF, NACME, Technology Student Association (TSA), Health Occupations Student Association (HOSA), International Baccalaureate (IB), New Tech Network, Automation Federation, and Skills USA. PLTW is able to provide the most cutting-edge, comprehensive STEM education programs and cultivate a larger STEM community by creating a collaborative network. By communicating and sharing our creativity, ideas, and knowledge, we create a stronger organization and a more meaningful experience for students, parents, educators, and all those who play a part in making PLTW successful.

Taking a page from the academic work of Professor Michael Porter, of the Harvard Business School, and his concept of "shared value,"—the concept that policies and practices that enhance the competitiveness of a company will simultaneously advance the economic and social conditions in the communities in which it operates—Project Lead The Way's mission is advanced by out-standing partnerships with America's leading companies who share concerns about education and developing a highly-skilled and well-educated workforce.[135] Companies such as Chevron, Lockheed Martin, General Motors, Autodesk, Amgen, Toyota,

Dow Chemical, Bemis, Pentair, Cummins, John Deere, 3M, Cargill, SunPower, Dart, Cerner, Rockwell Collins, Rockwell Automation, Intel, SAIC, Rolls Royce, and many others are engaged in this work. Foundations such as the Kern Family Foundation, Ewing Marion Kauffman Foundation, Lilly Endowment, Charles and Lynn Schusterman Foundation, Society of Manufacturing Engineers Education Foundation, John S. and James L. Knight Foundation, and many others provide substantial support to schools. For example, the KC STEM Alliance has created a model regional collaboration to support PLTW programs in most Kansas City metro-area schools.

Chevron is an excellent example of a company that is creating shared value by leading the way in changing America's STEM education and professional development landscape. As one of the company's key strategies, Chevron partners with PLTW, NextEd (formerly LEED) and PLTW Affiliates San Diego State University, Cal Poly Pomona, California State University East Bay, and the largest supplier of engineers to Silicon Valley, San Jose State University, to increase the number of STEM professionals throughout California. Chevron encourages students' interest in STEM disciplines by increasing student access to PLTW programs. They have also created extracurricular opportunities including the Chevron Engineering Design Challenge—a competition for student teams centered on a design problem. This partnership also facilitates the sharing of successful practices and informs policymakers on ways to improve STEM education.

Chevron recently announced a multi-year, multi-million dollar investment to implement PLTW programs nationwide. This type of collaborative effort has incredible potential for scalable impact.

Another example of a PLTW partnership that has significant shared value is with Toyota, Bluegrass Community and Technical College, the University of Kentucky (PLTW Affiliate), and the Kentucky Association of Manufacturers. This model is a scalable solution addressing the STEM education and workforce needs of Kentucky. The University of Kentucky trains teachers and helps support more than 100 PLTW schools in the Commonwealth. Toyota actively recruits from these schools so it can access the workforce it needs. As Toyota's Dennis Parker put it: "PLTW did not find us, we found them! PLTW is the premier STEM program in the U.S. and the world to Toyota officials for two main reasons. Students are engaged every day in problem solving activities and work every day in teams! We also know that PLTW maintains its up-to-date curriculum, provides a unique and rigorous teacher professional development model, and their schools are certified for quality." PLTW students who are recruited to Toyota enter the Advanced Manufacturing Technician (AMT) program and start working toward a two-year degree with the Bluegrass Community and Technical College offered on Toyota's campus, specially designed for more effective technical education. Toyota and the Kentucky Association of Manufacturers have outlined a model that not only works for Kentucky but is being expanded to other states with Toyota operations. These industry and educational leaders are working together to meet local and regional education and economic development needs. Toyota is now implementing the AMT program at all their U.S. manufacturing facilities.

By collaborating with K-12 schools, colleges, universities, foundations, community organizations, and businesses, we can signal to students the importance of STEM education. We can engage students in rigorous studies, create excitement about STEM careers, and make learning relevant by presenting real-world problems and utilizing the same industry-standard technology used by STEM professionals—sparking curiosity, creating a laboratory for innovation and discovery, and inspiring an entrepreneurial mindset.

However, PLTW is most effective where there are strong community champions. Through local partnership teams, schools work intimately with their local STEM community to (1) select

PLTW courses that align with the local or regional economy, (2) provide relevant field trips and speakers for PLTW courses, (3) create workplace experiences for students with industry partners, and (4) serve as mentors for students–especially on projects where the local community has specific subject matter expertise. PLTW has found that most businesses and STEM professionals take great pride in their local communities and relate well to the concept of creating home-grown talent.

The point is, the people working with our schools and students are creating shared value. They care about their companies and their jobs, yes; but they also care about building a stronger workforce. Like most Americans, they care about their communities and they care about their country. But, they are not standing idle. They are leveraging their resources to help solve America's STEM crisis.

Results

PLTW measures student knowledge, skills, and habits of mind through nationally administered End of Course Assessments and project-based assessments. Data are collected and analyzed to evaluate program effectiveness and to provide direction to PLTW on how to improve or modify the curriculum or provide additional teacher training. PLTW, in partnership with PLTW State Leaders—those in leadership positions who actively promote PLTW in their respective states—and PLTW University Affiliates, also has a national school certification process and training for counselors and administrators designed to ensure program fidelity and quality.

While formal course assessments can go a long way in evaluating student performance and aptitude, we must also evaluate collaboration and leadership skills, creativity, and workplace experiences beyond the classroom. The Innovation Portal makes it possible. Developed by PLTW, that Innovation Portal is an open access, 24/7 dynamic online tool that enables students to create, maintain, and share digital portfolios that can be used for classes, college admissions, and job applications. Students can invite guests to the portal for collaboration and evaluation purposes.

Nevertheless, the salient and fair question is: "does it all work?" Several independent research studies reveal that PLTW students out-perform their peers in school, and are more focused on attending college than non-PLTW students. In college, PLTW students persist and perform at higher levels than their non-PLTW peers. In general, research studies indicate that PLTW students are more likely to consider careers as scientists, technology experts, engineers, mathematicians, healthcare providers, and researchers compared to their non-PLTW peers. The studies are unique in design. Some studies are regionally or locally focused within school districts, others examine and track PLTW alumni and their performance in college.

In November 2012, Dr. Robert Tai, Associate Professor at the University of Virginia, and his team of researchers collected and analyzed more than thirty studies and reports on PLTW. Dr. Tai's report states, "Research on PLTW programs across the U.S. offers evidence that PLTW contributes to raising student achievement and motivation in science and engineering, both of which are essential to success in these career fields."[136]

A recent six-year longitudinal study from Texas State University found that PLTW students scored significantly higher on the state's eleventh grade mathematics assessment, a higher percentage met the college-ready criterion, a higher percentage enrolled in Texas higher education institutions, and the non-college-bound PLTW students earned higher wages.

If you need further evidence, visit a PLTW school. Consider Pike Central High School in Petersburg, Indiana. Pike County is a rural community in south central Indiana. Pike Central High School students were emotionally moved by several natural disasters they saw in the media. So, they collaborated to develop an emergency shelter with solar power and a water filtration system.

The students—Jessica, Colton, Anna, among others in the class won first place for the project at MIT and presented the shelter to President Obama at the White House Science Fair in 2012.

More than fifty percent of Pike Central students are enrolled in PLTW courses, including both Biomedical Sciences and Engineering programs. On a recent visit to the school, students presented a range of projects including the award-winning emergency shelter, mobile apps for southwest Indiana businesses, a method for killing E. coli bacteria in water, and a Humvee that the students transformed into a remote-controlled vehicle.

The Pike County Chamber of Commerce and Economic Growth and Development Council believe in and support PLTW. Paul Lake, the executive director of the Economic Growth and Development Council, stated, "PLTW is important not just to Pike County, but to Indiana and the nation as a whole. The best and brightest are coming up through school, and we need to figure out a way to foster their entrepreneurialism and innovation in our communities, rather than sending them off to a large city to chase a job."

Examine Gulliver Preparatory School in Miami, Florida. After several devastating natural disasters, the country of Haiti remains the poorest country in the Western hemisphere, while holding the highest number of infant mortalities, mainly due to the prevalence of waterborne diseases and inaccessibility to clean, potable water. Engineering students at Gulliver Preparatory School wanted to help, so they designed and manufactured a clean energy water filtration system. Students discovered in the aftermath of the 2010 earthquake that the UV lights, wires, and the necessary electrical outlet to support the purifier were too complex and fragile. After numerous design modifications and improvements, they developed a new water purification system that did not require an external energy source.

Not only did Gulliver win the Conrad Foundation's Spirit of Innovation Challenge, students Ian, Laura, and their classmates, along with Master Teacher Claude Charron, were presented with the Heart of Haiti award recognizing the impact their work was having on the people of Haiti.

It is through world-class curriculum, high-quality professional development, an engaged network, and delivering positive results that PLTW is widely recognized as the nation's preeminent STEM solution. U.S. Secretary of Education Arne Duncan called PLTW a "great model of the new CTE succeeding all across the country," and *Pathways to Prosperity: Meeting the Challenge of Preparing Young American's for the 21st Century*, from Harvard University, called PLTW a "model for 21st-century career and technical education."

Yes, PLTW works. However, only through the continued promotion of these ideals can PLTW continue engaging new students and help them meet their full potential. America's students who succeed in STEM-related fields will transform this country, and given the opportunity, they will transform the world.

The stakes are high!

5

Conclusion

This book is not about averting a crisis; it is about solving one. The work of reforming our education system, generally, and the way we teach and inspire STEM education, specifically, has never been more urgent. We face precarious economic times, we have a too-high unemployment rate, and yet we have millions of jobs unfilled in America because of a lack of skilled and interested talent to fill them. But, we do not have a people shortage. We have a STEM skills gap because we have an expectations and aspirations gap. And we have those gaps because we do not expect enough of our students, and our students do not expect enough of themselves. That is why our greatest threat to economic prosperity is, right now, not our inability to solve these problems but rather our commitment to high expectations for all students, inspiring intellectual curiosity, and building a nation of collaborative problem solvers, critical thinkers, innovators, and entrepreneurs. While I have highlighted the problems we have and the challenges we face, inspired and engaged students will solve most of these factual problems over the course of the next generation—but *only if we do our part by inspiring and engaging them today.*

Science, technology, engineering, and math education are essential for our students and our country. These areas are where the jobs are and where our future lies. It is where American greatness lies. It is no mistake or coincidence that the minds that helped shape our country, from Thomas Jefferson to Benjamin Franklin, were the same minds that gave us inventions and designs, from the spherical sundial and swivel chair to the moldboard of least resistance, from the cipher wheel to maps of the Gulf Stream and bifocals and swim fins.[137]

I implore parents and principals, teachers and superintendents: focus on STEM. Make it exciting, but also rigorous and relevant. Connect students with great role models. I know it can be done— I see pockets of excellence every day. But, pockets of excellence are not good enough. We have to create a system of excellence. Do not make excuses or confuse budget constraints with priorities—in other words, we invest in what we believe is important. Do not settle for the minimum that qualifies to check the STEM box. Demand the best for your students and deliver it to all of them.

The *Wall Street Journal* recently put it this way: We face a future of either "rapid innovation driven by robotic manufacturing, 3-D printing and cloud computing" or one of "job losses, stagnant wages and rising income inequality."[138] Northwestern University economist Robert Gordon goes so far as to say all the great inventions are behind us[139]— we cannot accept that. Professor Gordon illustrates his point this way: he asks audiences what their choice would be if they could keep everything invented up until 2002 or keep everything invented after—his examples, the indoor toilet versus the smart phone. He says the indoor toilet was the major innovation, changing the way people live while the smart phone was merely a refinement of something already invented. The *Wall Street Journal* asked the same question of its readers. The response? Seventy-one percent would rather have their smart phone than an indoor toilet, while twenty-nine percent would rather have the toilet.[140]

There are, of course, people in the world who do not have indoor plumbing but can read the *Wall Street Journal* on their phones. And there are people who, I imagine, have indoor plumbing but not a smart phone and get along just fine. The question, the option, misses the point. The point is smart phones changed the world—from thought to communication. Indoor plumbing changed life for the better, too. But as humans, we truly can get along without either. We may not carry on well, or as happily or as prosperously as we would like, but we would carry on. Now the words "greatness" and "best" make sense. We can live without toilets but are we not better off for having them? We can live without smart phones but are not most of us more productive with them? We can have both indoor toilets and smart phones and recognize that we are better off for both.

And we can do one other thing, too: recognize that we have no idea what we may be capable of inventing five and ten years down the road. People may ask about the next Internet, but that is like taking the year of 1980 and asking about the next word processor— the Internet was nowhere on the scene of people's imaginations. The distance between the 1987 5k memory word processor and the way in which I am writing this book, and using the Internet for research along the way, is the distance in imagination and invention and discovery from the indoor toilet to the smart phone. The change in telephonic communications and electronic mail delivery represents a world of difference that took place within the span of a decade, from 1990 to 2000 for example. We simply cannot fathom what we are capable of creating or solving.

My last anecdote: Erica Malloy is a Project Lead The Way science teacher at Marshalltown High School in Iowa. The *Times Republican* newspaper pictures her with a broad and bright smile and describes her excitement about her new biomedical sciences curriculum: "Students will be matching DNA, examining genetic diseases, doing mock crime scene investigations and utilizing a ton of technology as part of the new class."[141] "It's a lot of what they would be doing in a college lab, but they are getting this at the high school level," Malloy said. "When they go to college they will be ahead of the game." In addition to all this, the local medical and surgical center will be sending professionals into the classroom to help inspire and train students. Ms. Malloy's students will be ahead of the game not just for college, but for life.

There are several thousand schools with classrooms like this in America today. That is the good news. The challenging news—the opportunity—is that in America today there are over 50 million school students, public and private, and nearly 130,000 schools.[142] We have a lot of work to do to reach all of them. But there is a concerted call of concern now from industry and government. I want to impress how critical it is that parents and educators join that call. Demand can, after all, drive supply.

I have avoided using the phrase "Sputnik moment" in talking about the need for a STEM revolution. I think the idea of a "Sputnik moment" is trite and has been used for too long without enough action. One looks at the reams of studies on education reforms, the totality of education experiments, and the trillions of dollars invested in our education system over the past several decades, and we can fairly say we have tried any number of moon shots. Meanwhile, our scores have remained flat—at best—over the same period. Instead of calling for such another moment, as so many studies do, I suggest we simply get to work with what has proven to work. And, we must make these programs available to all students.

The elements of having an entire system of schools with safe atmospheres, clear missions, good to great teachers, solid leadership, substantive evaluations (for both teachers and students), parental involvement, and a sense of community is just not that difficult.[143] What will be difficult will be sustaining our national success and building our children and our students' futures if we do not demand and employ these elements now.

If we believe in American exceptionalism, if we believe we are the last best hope of mankind, if we believe we are the country the tempest-tossed run to, if we believe we are a shining city on a hill, it is time to be honest with ourselves. A revolution in our thinking and practice of teaching science, technology, engineering, and math is, quite simply, our moral and economic imperative of the day. The crisis is here, in the present. We have no idea what and who we are losing by the day, how many potential Mark Zuckerbergs, Steve Jobses, or Marissa Mayers we are turning off from STEM fields each year or each day. We can marvel at the state of our technology today and such achievements unimaginable to most people just a few years ago, such as 3-D printers, Google Glass, Smart Watches, and autonomous vehicles. And technology changes rapidly. As recently as 2006, there were no iPhones, as recently as 2009 there were no iPads. Today those two products generate over seventy percent of Apple's revenue.[144]

Today, many of us have a GPS system in our car that has changed driving entirely. Is that a new invention or a refinement of cartography or the American Automobile Association's TripTiks? The question is irrelevant. A short twenty years ago most people were still asking their friends for directions to places they had been or lived in order to travel there. Now we go to remote places in our cars without even thinking about how we would have arrived there or mapped it as we once had to...without much accuracy.

As I say above, we have no idea what we are capable of, what we are missing, and what tomorrow could be like with a serious effort aimed at excellence in STEM education. My concern is not whether all the great innovations have been invented, it is whether we will continue to invent at the pace we have in the past. It's not as if all the diseases have been cured, nor that we can even imagine how much better our lives can be when or if the next Internet is invented.

I have long respected outsiders' views of America. They often see us better than we see ourselves. Thus, a speech the former Prime Minister of Australia, Julia Gillard, delivered to a Joint Session of Congress in Washington, D.C. in 2011 was too-little noticed, but it touched my heart as strongly as any I have heard in recent memory. I close with it:

> Our future growth relies on competitiveness and innovation, skills and productivity, and these in turn rely on the education of our people...

In both our countries, true friends stick together, in both our countries, real mates talk straight. So as a friend I urge you only this: be worthy to your own best traditions. Be bold. In 1942, John Curtin—my predecessor, my country's great wartime leader—looked to America. I still do...

The eyes of the world are still upon you. Your city on a hill cannot be hidden. Your brave and free people have made you the masters of recovery and reinvention.

As I stand in this cradle of democracy, I see a nation that has changed the world and known remarkable days. I firmly believe you are the same people who amazed me when I was a small girl by landing on the moon. On that great day I believed Americans could do anything.

I believe that still.[145]

The great reform and adventure begins today. I would like to think this book has convinced the adults—parents, teachers, principals, elected officials, corporate and community leaders. We must now convince our children.

Endnotes

1 National Assessment of Educational Progress. NAEP - Nation's Report Card. http://nationsreportcard.gov/reading_math_g12_2013/#/whatknowledge.

2 Ibid.

3 Ibid.

4 "An International Education Test." *The New York Times*. December 7, 2010. http://www.nytimes.com/imagepages/2010/12/07/education/07education_graph.html?ref=education 5.

5 Organisation for Economic Co-operation and Development. "PISA 2012 Results." OECD Better Policies for Better Lives. http://www.oecd.org/pisa/keyfindings/pisa-2012-results.htm.

6 "The Human Wealth of Nations." *Wall Street Journal*. December 3, 2013. http://online.wsj.com/news/articles/SB10001424052702304355104579 236150801599552#printMode.

7 Dillon, Sam. "Top Test Scores From Shanghai Stun Educators." *The New York Times*. December 7, 2010. http://www.nytimes.com/2010/12/07/education/07education.html?pagewanted=all&_r=1&.

8 National Assessment of Educational Progress. "What Every Parent Should Know About NAEP." National Center for Educational Statistics. http://nces.ed.gov/nationsreportcard/pdf/parents/2012469.pdf.

9 National Assessment of Educational Progress. "NAEP - Nation's Report Card Home." NAEP - Nation's Report Card.

10 Ibid.

11 The most recent NAEP report for 12th-graders is 2010; the most recent NAEP report for fourth- and eighth- graders is 2013.

12 Bennett, William. "STEM Education That Works." *Wall Street Journal*. June 14, 2013. http://online.wsj.com/article/PR-CO-20130614-905532.html.

13 The Nation's Report Card. "Science 2009 National Assessment of Educational Progress at Grades 4, 8, and 12." National Center for Educational Statistics. http://nces.ed.gov/nationsreportcard/pdf/main2009/2011451.pdf.

14 The Nation's Report Card. "Science 2011 National Assessment of Educational Progress at Grade 8." National Center for Educational Statistics. http://nces.ed.gov/nationsreportcard/pdf/main2011/2012465.pdf.

15 "Science 2009 National Assessment of Educational Progress at Grades 4, 8, and 12."

16 "Report to the President: Engage To Excel: Producing One Million Additional College Graduates With Degrees In Science, Technology, Engineering, And Mathematics." The White House. February 1, 2012. http://www.whitehouse.gov/sites/default/files/microsites/ostp/pcast-engage-to-excel-final_feb.pdf.

17 My College Options STEM Connector 2012-2013. "Where Are the STEM Students? What Are Their Career Interests? Where Are the STEM Jobs?" STEM Connector. http://www.stemconnector.org/sites/default/files/store/STEM-Students-STEM-Jobs-Executive-Summary.pdf.

18 The Nation's Report Card. "Grade 12 Reading and Mathematics 2009 National and Pilot State Results." National Center for Educational Statistics. http://nces.ed.gov/nationsreportcard/pdf/main2009/2011455.pdf.

19 "Science 2009 National Assessment of Educational Progress at Grades 4, 8, and 12."

20 "STEMtistic: Proficient at Math, but Not Interested." Change The Equation. http://changetheequation.org/stemtistic-proficient-math-not-interested-0.

21 Sheehy, Kelsey. "Colleges Fight to Retain Interest of STEM Majors." US News and World Report. June 18, 2013. http://www.usnews.com/education/best-colleges/articles/2013/06/18/ colleges-fight-to-retain-interest-of-stem-majors.

22 My College Options STEM Connector 2012-2013.

23 "Reagan Quotes." PBS. http://www.pbs.org/wgbh/
americanexperience/features/general-article/reagan-quotes/.

24 Solzhenitsyn, Aleksandr. "Words of Warning to the Western World."
August 14, 2002. http://lib.ru/PROZA/SOLZHENICYN/s_word_
engl.txt_with-big-pictures.html.

25 The Editors of Encyclopædia Britannica. "Thomas Wolfe."
Encyclopedia Britannica. http://www.britannica.com/topic/646559/
supplemental-information.

26 "Reagan Quotes."

27 In writing about the "Carter years" and mentioning the presidents
and candidates, I mean to make no political judgments—simply
to jog memories—I have long believed presidents have but a small
responsibility and effect on employment rates.

28 NPA Services Inc. "United States Misery Index." US Misery Index.
http://www.miseryindex.us/indexbymonth.aspx?type=UR.

29 Ibid.

30 Ibid.

31 Zuckerman, Mortimer. "Mort Zuckerman: A Jobless Recovery is a
Phony Recovery." *Wall Street Journal.* July 15, 2013.

32 Portlock, Sarah, and Jeffrey Sparshott. " GDP Revisions Make
Recovery Look Better, Recession Not as Bad." *Wall Street Journal.*
July 31, 2013. http://blogs.wsj.com/economics/2013/07/31/gdp-
revisions-make-recovery-look-better-recession-not-as-bad/.

33 Amadeo, Kimberly. "US GDP Growth." About. http://useconomy.
about.com/od/grossdomesticproduct/a/US-GDP-Growth.htm.

34 House, Jonathan. "U.S. Economy Shrinks by Most in Five Years." *Wall
Street Journal.* June 25, 2014. http://online.wsj.com/articles/u-s-
gdp-contracted-at-2-9-pace-in-first-quarter-1403699600.

35 Ibid.

36 Ibid.

37 Leubsdorf, Ben. "GDP Expanded at 4.2% Rate in Second Quarter."
The Wall Street Journal. August 28, 2014. http://online.wsj.com/
articles/gdp-expanded-at-4-2-rate-in-second-quarter-1409229416.

38 Mitchell, Josh. "Student-Loan Debt Tops $1 Trillion." *The Wall Street Journal*. March 22, 2012. http://online.wsj.com/news/articles/SB 10001424052702303812904577295930047604846?mg=reno64-wsj&url=http://online.wsj.com/article/SB10001424052702303812 9045772959930047604846.html.

39 O'Shaughnessy, Lynn. "College Grads Overconfident in Job Prospects." CBS News. May 9, 2013. http://www.cbsnews.com/news/college-grads-overconfident-in-job-prospects/.

40 Koba, Mark. "Job Picture Looks Bleak for 2013 College Grads." CNBC. April 26, 2013. http://www.cnbc.com/id/100673848.

41 Shierholz, Heidi, Natalie Sabadish, and Nicholas Finio. "The Class of 2013." Economic Policy Institute. April 10, 2013. http://www.epi.org/publication/class-of-2013-graduates-job-prospects/40/.

42 Neal, Meghan. "Half College Grads Can't Find Full-Time Work, Studies Show." *Daily News*. May 10, 2012. http://www.nydailynews.com/news/money/college-grads-find-full-time-work-study-shows-article-1.1075873#ixzz2bP9BlZsW.

43 Koba, Mark.

44 Ibid.

45 Porter, Eduardo. "Dropping Out of College and Paying the Price." *The New York Times*. June 25, 2013. http://www.nytimes.com/2013/06/26/business/economy/dropping-out-of-college-and-paying-the-price.html?pagewanted=all&_r=0.

46 Richmond, Emily. "High School Graduation Rate Hits 40-Year Peak in the U.S." *The Atlantic*. June 6, 2013. http://www.theatlantic.com/national/archive/2013/06/high-school-graduation-rate-hits-40-year-peak-in-the-us/276604/.

47 Bennett, William J. and Wilezol, David, *Is College Worth It?* Thomas Nelson, 2013. P. VII.

48 "H1B Visa Application." H1B Visa. http://www.h1bvisa.org/.

49 Khan, Huma. "Are Americans Losing High-Skilled Jobs to Foreigners?" ABC News. February 1, 2012. http://abcnews.go.com/blogs/politics/2012/02/are-americans-losing-high-skilled-jobs-to-foreigners/.

50 Calderon, Sara. "STEM Visa Immigration Reform Most Likely to Benefit Asians." Politic 365. January 31, 2013. http://politic365. com/2013/01/31/stem-visa-immigration-reform-most-likely-to-benefit-asians-not-latinos/.

51 President's Council of Advisors on Science and Technology. "Report to the President: Prepare and Inspire: K-12 Education in Science, Technology, Engineering, and Math(STEM) for America's Future." White House. September 1, 2010. http://www.whitehouse.gov/sites/ default/files/microsites/ostp/pcast-stemed-report.pdf.

52 Ibid.

53 West, Darrell. "Improving STEM Education in the United States." Brookings. September 12, 2011. http://www.brookings.edu/blogs/ up-front/posts/2011/09/12-stem-west.

54 Weihua, Chen. "PEW Poll: China Will Top US." *China Daily.* July 19, 2013. http://usa.chinadaily.com.cn/epaper/2013-07/19/ content_16798933.htm.

55 Ibid.

56 Kurlantzick, Joshua. "China Falling? Not So Fast." *Bloomberg Businessweek.* June 28, 2013. http://www.businessweek.com/ articles/2013-06-28/china-falling-not-so-fast.

57 Arcega, Mil. "US 2nd Quarter GDP - Lackluster, But Better Than Expected." Voice of America. August 1, 2013. http://www.voanews. com/content/us-second-quarter-gdp-lackluster-but-better-than-expected/1717104.html.

58 Dillon, Sam.

59 Strauss, Valerie. "New Data on Public Education Released." *Washington Post.* October 12, 2012. http://www.washingtonpost. com/blogs/answer-sheet/wp/2012/10/12/new-data-on-public-education-released/.

60 Conrad, Cameron. "U.S. Education Spending Tops Other Countries." Students First. July 3, 2013. http://www.studentsfirst.org/blog/ entry/u.s.-education-spending-tops-other-countries.

61 Gorman, Christine. "Advances in Science Drive Economic Growth." *Scientific American*. July 26, 2012. http://blogs.scientificamerican. com/observations/2012/07/26/science-drives-economic-growth/.

62 "President Hockfield Stresses Innovation in Speech to U.S. Governors." *MIT News*. July 15, 2011. http://newsoffice.mit. edu/2011/nga-conference-hockfield-0715.

63 Ibid.

64 The story of GM's bankruptcy and recovery is complicated by a great many political judgments, but this Forbes Magazine account is but one of the explanations on how GM recovered through ingenuity as well as public investment: http://www.forbes.com/ sites/danbigman/2013/10/30/how-general-motors-was-really-savedthe-untold-true-story-of-the-most-important-bankruptcy-in-u-shistory/

65 Spangler, Todd. "Dan Akerson Meets with Members of Congress to Boast of GM's Resurgence." *Detroit Free Press*. March 21, 2013. http://www.freep.com/article/20130321/ BUSINESS0101/130321039/.

66 Dumaine, Brian. "FedEx CEO Fred Smith on ... Everything." *Fortune Magazine*. May 11, 2012. http://fortune.com/2012/05/11/fedex-ceo-fred-smith-on-everything/.

67 Adkins, Rodney. "America Desperately Needs More STEM STudents. Here's How to Get Them." *Forbes*. July 9, 2012. http://www.forbes. com/sites/forbesleadershipforum/2012/07/09/america-desperately-needs-more-stem-students-heres-how-to-get-them/.

68 Information Technology Industry Council. "Private Sector Leaders Committed to Efforts Focused on Science, Technology, Engineering, and Math (STEM) Education." *PR Newswire*. http:// www.prnewswire.com/news-releases/private-sector-leaders-committed-to-efforts-focused-on-science-technology-engineering-and-math-stem-education-71572447.html.

69 "About Change the Equation." Change the Equation. http:// changetheequation.org/about-change-equation.

70 President's Council of Advisors on Science and Technology.

71 Ibid.

72 West, Darrell. "Improving STEM Education in the United States." Brookings. September 12, 2011. http://www.brookings.edu/blogs/up-front/posts/2011/09/12-stem-west.

73 Black Point Policy Solutions, LLC. "Building a Science, Technology, Engineering, and Math Education Agenda." National Governors Association. http://www.nga.org/files/live/sites/NGA/files/pdf/1112STEMGUIDE. PDF.

74 Rosen, Linda. "STEM Is Where the Jobs Are at." STEM Blog. May 21, 2012. http://blog.stemconnector.org/linda-rosen-stem-where-jobs-are.

75 Bennett & Wilezol, Supra. P. 92.

76 Ibid., P.93.

77 Ibid.

78 Ibid.

79 Ibid., P. 95.

80 Bui, Quoctrung. "What's Your Major? 4 Decades Of College Degrees, In 1 Graph." NPR. May 9, 2014. http://www.npr.org/blogs/money/2014/05/09/310114739/whats-your-major-four-decades-of-college-degrees-in-1-graph.

81 Ibid.

82 Ibid.

83 Ibid.

84 Ibid.

85 Ibid.

86 Langdon, David, George McKittrick, Mark Doms, David Beede, and Beethika Kahn. "STEM: Good Jobs Now and for the Future." Economics and Statistics Administration. http://www.esa.doc.gov/sites/default/files/reports/documents/stemfinalyjuly14_1.pdf.

87 National Governors Association, the Council of Chief State School Officers, and Achieve, Inc. "Benchmarking for Success: Ensuring

U.S. Students Receive AWorld-Class Education." http://www.
edweek.org/media/benchmakring for success dec 2008 final.pdf.

88 Hanushek, Eric A., Peterson, Paul E., Woessmann, Ludgar.
Endangering Prosperity-A Global View of the American School,
Brookings Institution Press. 2013, pp. 11-12.

89 GreatSchools Staff. "Thinking Globally." GreatSchools. http://www.
greatschools.org/students/academic-skills/2458-Eric-Hanushek-
interview.gs?page=all.

90 Hanushek, Peterson, Woessmann. op.cit. pp.12 & 63.

91 The National Commission on Excellence in Education. "A Nation
at Risk: The Imperative for Educational Reform A Report to the
Nation and the Secretary of Education United States Department of
Education." Data Center. April 1, 1983. http://datacenter.spps.org/
uploads/sotw_a_nation_at_risk_1983.pdf.

92 Ibid.

93 Finn, Chester. "The Case for Saturday School." *Wall Street Journal.*
March 20, 2010. http://online.wsj.com/news/articles/SB1000142405
2748704207504575130073852829574?mg=reno64-wsj&url=http://
online.wsj.com/article/SB10001424052748704207504575130073852
829574.html.

94 Ibid.

95 Ibid.

96 Milken, Michael. "Where's Sputnik? Summoning the Will to Create
the Next American Century." *The Milken Institute Review: A Journal
of Economic Policy,* 2011. http://www.mikemilken.com/wheres-
sputnik.pdf.

97 Gates, Bill. "How Teacher Development Could Revolutionize
Our Schools." *Washington Post.* February 28, 2011. http://www.
washingtonpost.com/wp-dyn/content/article/2011/02/27/
AR2011022702876.html?hpid=news-col-blog.

98 Bennett, William. "For Superior Teachers, Reward Excellence."
CNN. March 7, 2011. http://www.cnn.com/2011/OPINION/03/02/
bennett.education.teachers.unions/index.html.

99 Ibid.

100 McKinsey and Company. "Closing the Talent Gap: Attracting and Retaining Top-third Graduates to Careers and Teaching." McKinsey on Society. September 1, 2010.

101 Ibid.

102 Ibid.

103 Ibid.

104 "Teach for America Press Kit." Teach for America. June 19, 2012.

105 MetLife. "The MetLife Survey of the American Teacher." Metropolitan Life Insurance Company. http://files.eric.ed.gov/fulltext/ED530021.pdf.

106 Hanushek, Eric. "Valuing Good Teachers: How Much Is a Good Teacher Worth?" Hoover Institute Stanford University. January 1, 2011. http://hanushek.stanford.edu/publications/valuing-teachers-how-much-good-teacher-worth.

107 Moe, Michael, and Luben Pampulov. "Demography Is Density." Next Up: Insider Insights on the Growth Economy. June 26, 2011. http://mikemilken.com/pdfs/NextUp.pdf.

108 Sethna, Beheruz. "Messages From a Flattening World." University of West Georgia. May 1, 2006. http://www.westga.edu/president/messages_from_a_flattening_world.php.

109 "Family Structure and Children's Education." Family Facts. http://www.familyfacts.org/briefs/35/family-structure-and-childrens-education.

110 Drew, Christopher. "Why Science Majors Change Their Minds (It's Just So Darn Hard)." *The New York Times.* November 4, 2011. http://www.nytimes.com/2011/11/06/education/edlife/why-science-majors-change-their-mind-its-just-so-darn-hard.html?pagewanted=all&_r=0.

111 Ibid.

112 Ibid.

113 Ibid.

114 Pinker, Steven. "Science Is Not Your Enemy." *New Republic.* August 6, 2013. http://www.newrepublic.com/article/114127/science-not-enemy-humanities.

115 Ibid.

116 Ibid.

117 Bennett, William. "U.S Lag in Science, Math a Disaster in the Making." CNN. February 9, 2012. http://www.cnn.com/2012/02/09/opinion/bennett-stem-education.

118 Ibid.

119 Hrabowski, Freeman. "4 Pillars of College Success in Science." TED. February 1, 2013. http://www.ted.com/talks/freeman_hrabowski_4_pillars_of_college_success_in_science.

120 Cordoza, Kavitha. "Chronic Absenteeism: Public School's Forgotten Problem?" WAMU American University Radio. June 1, 2012. http://wamu.org/programs/metro_connection/12/06/01/chronic_absenteeism_public_schools_forgotten_problem.

121 Adkins, Rodney. "America Desperately Needs More STEM STudents. Here's How to Get Them." *Forbes.* July 9, 2012. http://www.forbes.com/sites/forbesleadershipforum/2012/07/09/america-desperately-needs-more-stem-students-heres-how-to-get-them/.

122 Tai, Robert. "An Examination of the Research Literature on Project Lead the Way." Project Lead the Way. November 1, 2012. http://www.pltw.org/sites/default/files/PLTW DR.TAI - brochure_pages.pdf.

123 Ibid.

124 "Exposure to Engineering Doubles Teens' Career Interest." Intel Newsroom. December 6, 2011. http://newsroom.intel.com/community/intel_newsroom/blog/2011/12/06/exposure-to-engineering-doubles-teens-career-interest.

125 Ibid.

126 Steel, David. "This Is How You Make Kids Love Math." *Washington Post.* June 4, 2012. http://www.washingtonpost.com/national/on-innovations/this-is-how-you-make-kids-love-math/2012/06/04/gJQAw38XDV_story.html.

127 "The STEM Crisis." Nation Math Science Initiative. https://www. nms.org/AboutNMSI/TheSTEMCrisis.aspx.

128 Ibid.

129 Abdul-Amin, Jamaal. "Experts Differ on Route to Getting Talented Teachers to Most Challenged Schools." *Diverse.* April 4, 2013. http://diverseeducation.com/article/52410/.

130 Soave, Robby, and Rachel Stoltzfoos. "Here Is the Conservative Defense of Common Core." The Daily Caller. March 12, 2014. http://dailycaller.com/2014/03/12/here-is-the-conservative-defense-of-common-core/.

131 Booth, Ryan. "A Conservative Defense of Common Core." *The Hayride.* May 1, 2013. http://thehayride.com/2013/05/a-conservative-defense-of-common-core/.

132 Ibid.

133 Blow, Charles M. "The Common Core and the Common Good." *The New York Times.* August 21, 2013. http://www.nytimes. com/2013/08/22/opinion/blow-the-common-core-and-the-common-good.html?src=me&ref=general&_r=1&.

134 Porter-Magee, Kathleen. "Why Conservatives Should Support the Common Core." Thomas B. Fordham Institute. April 3, 2013. http://edexcellence.net/commentary/education-gadfly-daily/common-core-watch/2013/why-conservatives-should-support-the-common-core.html.

135 For more on "shared value," see: https://archive.harvardbusiness. org/cla/web/pl/product.seam?c=24811&i=25967&cs=e3c4e5ddc7e9 cb91d18872a098ee63b6

136 Tai, Robert. "An Examination of the Research Literature on Project Lead the Way." Project Lead the Way. November 1, 2012. http://www.pltw.org/sites/default/files/PLTW DR.TAI - brochure_pages.pdf.

137 Independence Hall Association. "Benjamin Franklin's Inventions, Discoveries, and Improvements." The Electric Ben Franklin. http://www.ushistory.org/franklin/info/inventions.htm.; Thomas Jefferson Foundation. "Jefferson's Inventions." The Monticello Classroom.

http://classroom.monticello.org/kids/resources/profile/235/
Jefferson-s-Inventions/.

138 Aeppel, Timothy. "Economists Debate: Has All the Important
Stuff Already Been Invented?" *Wall Street Journal.* June 15, 2014.
http://online.wsj.com/articles/economists-duel-over-idea-that-
technology-will-save-the-world-1402886301?KEYWORDS=econo.

139 Aeppel, Timothy. "If You Had to Choose: IPhone or Toilet?"
Wall Street Journal. June 14, 2014. http://blogs.wsj.com/
economics/2014/06/15/if-you-had-to-choose-iphone-or-
toilet/?KEYWORDS=best inventions.

140 Ibid.

141 Potter, Andrew. "'Exciting' Curriculum Helps MHS Lead the Way."
Times-Republican. July 27, 2013. http://www.timesrepublican.com/
page/content.detail/id/562380/- Exciting-curriculum-helps-MHS-
lead-the-way.html.

142 U.S. Department of Education, Institute of Education Sciences,
and National Center for Education Statistics. "Fast Facts." National
Center for Education Statistics. January 1, 2013. http://nces.ed.gov/
fastfacts/display.asp?id=372.

143 Bennett, William J., Chester E. Finn, Jr, and John T.E. Cribb, Jr.
*The Educated Child—A Parent's Guide from Preschool Through the
Eighth Grade.* New York: Free Press, 1999.

144 Cunningham, Andrew. "Apple Breaks Revenue, IPhone, and IPad
Records in Q1 of 2014." ARS Technica. January 27, 2014. http://
arstechnica.com/apple/2014/01/apple-breaks-revenue-iphone-and-
ipad-records-in-q1-of-2014/.

145 "Australia's Prime Minister Julia Gillard: 'There Is a Reason the
World Always Looks to America'" *Los Angeles Times Blog.* March
10, 2011. http://latimesblogs.latimes.com/washington/2011/03/
julia-gillard-australia-prime-minister-speech-to-u-s-congress-.
html.

Acknowledgments

This book would not have been possible without many people and organizations that take the issues I have written about so seriously. It is no exaggeration to say that without them, this country would be far less than what it is today. Each comes from diverse backgrounds and experiences, but they share a common belief about what our country needs to restore her greatness - greatness they have seen before, and greatness they want desperately to see again.

First, I would like to say "thank you" to Richard Blais, the late Richard Liebich, and the Charitable Leadership Foundation for their vision to develop and launch Project Lead The Way (PLTW).

PLTW's board of directors, past and present, is comprised of deeply committed, mission-driven leaders. For their extraordinary leadership and support, I want to thank our current directors Frank Zaffino, James Rahn, Dr. Mohammad Qayoumi, Kurt Liebich, Eunice Heath, Chris Bradshaw, John Calabrese and most recent former board members Dr. Hermann Viets, Marcia Peterson, and Dr. Joe Astroth.

Thank you, too, to PLTW's team of amazing educators and leaders. I admire their tireless work ethic and unwavering commitment to deliver a world-class education to all students in America. In particular, thank you to Kiley Adolph, Dr. Rex Bolinger, Jennifer Cahill, Dr. Andrea Croslyn, Jonathan Dilley, David Dimmett, Dorothy Gorman, Dr. Anne Jones, Carol Killworth, Cathy Lund, Valarie Osinski, and John Visconti.

And also to our great business and corporate partners, state leaders, university affiliates, and master teachers for their work throughout the country to promote PLTW, help train school personnel, and support thousands of PLTW teachers and students. Thank you to our thousands of dedicated teachers and school administrators who have embraced PLTW and are making it available to their students, they—like all great teacher and school administrators—do the second most important job in our country, after parents.

A special thanks goes to Bob and Pat Kern who want nothing more than to ignite curiosity in each child and ensure children get the education they deserve, and by extension, that America has the skilled workforce necessary to remain the greatest country in the world.

Thanks also to my great friend Seth Leibsohn for his tremendous support throughout the process of writing this book. He is one of the smartest individuals I know—and I, like many others, have a deep respect for Seth and his passion for education and our country.

Thank you to Christian Pinkston and the team at the Pinkston Group for their expert guidance in the publication of this book, and to Megan Trank and the team at Beaufort Books for their support.

Thank you to former U.S. Secretary of Education Dr. William J. Bennett for his friendship and wisdom.

Finally: My wife Jill, and sons Josh, Ryan, Drew, and Riley inspire me every day. I thank them for their unconditional support and love, and for allowing me to do this important work.

INDEX

A

absenteeism, 38
Achieve, Inc., 20
activity-, project-, and problem-based (APPB) learning, 57–58
Adkins, Rodney C., 16
Advanced Manufacturing Technician (AMT) program, 63
Advanced Placement program, 46
Affiliate institutions of PLTW, 60
Akerson, Dan, 16
America
  about, 7
  believing in our exceptionalism, 72–73
  cultural and familial deterrents to education reform, 32–33
  economic challenge to greatness, 8–10
  educational priorities, thinking, and structures, 33–36
  outsider's view of, 73–74
  staying competitive in the global economy, 12–15
  teacher quality and compensation, 29–32, 43–44, 45
AMT (Advanced Manufacturing Technician) program, 63
APPB (activity-, project-, and problem-based) learning, 57–58
archeology, 35–36
Asian countries' esteem for education, 32–33. See also specific Asian countries
assessments
  about, 46
  The Nation's Report Card (NAEP), 1, 3–4
  OECD PISA test, 2–3
  PLTW, 56, 64–65

B

Baesler, Kirsten, 46
Bennett, William J.
  on attending college, 11
  on deterioration of students during K-12 years, 3
  reforms for reinvigorating STEM education, 36–37
  on STEM vs. humanities courses, 18
  on teacher performance, 30
Blais, Richard, 52
Blank, Rebecca, 17–18
Blow, Charles, 47
Bluegrass Community and Technical College, Kentucky, 63
Brewer, Janice K., 47–48
Buckley, Jenni, 39
Bush, George W., 8

C

camps for summer learning, 28–29
Canada, 20–21
Carter, Jimmy, 8
Cato Institute on Trends in American Public Schooling Since 1970, 26
Center for American Progress, 43
Change the Equation, 17, 44, 52
Chevron, 62
Chevron Engineering Design Challenge, 62
children
  advice to, x, xii
  effect of single- or no-parent homes, 33
  front-loading STEM in pre- and grade school, 37, 40–42
  online resources for, 28, 44, 64
  PLTW Biomedical Sciences for high school students, 58
  PLTW Engineering for high school students, 58